Filipino Instant Pot® Cooking!

Yes! You CAN Do It!!

by Lola Nita Concepcion

Table of Contents

1. Dedication

To my supportive Filipino Family without which this
book would still be an
ethereal dream!

Maraming Salamat Po!
(Thank you very much!)

Lola Nita Concepcion

2. Mabuhay!

Can I tell you a secret?

In MY grandmother's day, cooking authentic Filipino food was an all-day affair. It wasn't uncommon to see my Grandmother up before sunrise, stoking a wood fire and preparing to settle in to an all-day cooking marathon.

Looking back, what amazes me the most is that she might only make one or two different recipes in those all-day affairs.

In our "hurry-hurry" world, such a luxury is unheard of.

Filipino foods are some of the world's finest, tasty and nutritious dishes. My challenge was how to distill the essence of these most excellent meals, retain their inherent wholesomeness, and still meet our modern lifestyles.

The answer lies in technology. **The Instant Pot®,** which to some is merely a glorified, automated pressure cooker, represents a whole new concept of cooking. It has the ability to compress time itself! A recipe that used to take 8-10 hours can now be accomplished perfectly in mere minutes.

I've taken my Grandmother's recipes and adapted them. You be the judge as to how well these recipes fit your family's lifestyle. I know they will easily satisfy your most fastidious family members!

Without further ado, let me get right into what you picked this book up for.....**THE RECIPES!!!!**

Adventures in Cooking!!

3. Instant Pot® Terminology

Instant Pot® cooking is a modern variation on an old theme. However, as with every technological advance, the meaning of words and descriptions tend to alter.

In this book, I will be referring to Instant Pot® settings that may not be exactly the same as on your Instant Pot®. while I have tried to make this book as generic possible, you may get confused.

To try to minimize this confusion, this section will describe the settings and functions on my Instant Pot®. Your "job" is to create a cross-reference to similar controls and functions on your Instant Pot®.

My Instant Pot® is an Instant Pot® DUO60 6 Qt 7-in-1 Multi-Use Programmable Pressure Cooker.

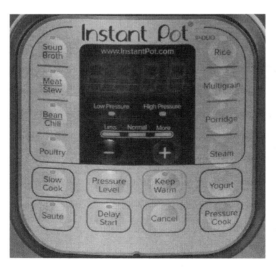

In some recipes, you may see a reference to a function called "Manual".

On my machine, this function is labeled "Pressure Cook".
It performs the same function as "Manual".
"Pressure Cook" and "Manual" are interchangeable.

Pressure Release Methods

There are two types of pressure release methods referenced in this cookbook.

1. **Normal Pressure Release (NPR)** method allows the Instant Pot®'s internal pressure to fall naturally, and the steam to re-condense. The NPR method starts when the Instant Pot® competes its cooking cycle and turns off (assuming you've selected ["Warm" off] when you set the pot up). NPR is a waiting period, typically between 5 and 20 minutes, depending on the recipe. At the end of the NPR period, you will open the steam vent and release any residual pressure and steam.
2. **Quick Release (QR)** method is when the pot completes its cooking cycle, you manually open the steam vent immediately, allowing the pressure and steam to vent. This method is dangerous: the escaping steam will scald. Don't have any part of your body in the path of the escaping steam.

In both methods, wait until the pressure indicating pin drops down before attempting to open the lid.

Cooking Program Options

Depending on your Instant Pot® model there are a variety of pre-programmed buttons for easy use. Here is a listing of the programs which are available on my IP-DUO60 model.

PRESSURE COOK – This is the most versatile setting, and one that gets the most use. The temperature, pressure levels, and cooking times, all can be controlled through the buttons on the control panel. For example, press the "Pressure Level" button to adjust the pressure level and the "+/-" buttons to change the cooking time.

SOUP/BROTH – This relatively low temperature setting (at 230°F) creates soups at a slow simmer. For vegetarian soups, use the **Less** mode; for soups containing meat, use the **Normal** mode; for artisan soups that requires longer cook times, such as rich bone broth, use the **More** mode.

MEAT/STEW – This mode is designed primarily for cooking cuts of meat that call for high pressure and low temperatures. For a "rare" texture, use the **Less** mode; for a very tender meat texture, use the **Normal** mode; for fall-off-the bone texture, use the **More** mode. You can cook meat at a low 230°F on "**Less**" for 20 minutes, "**Normal**" for 35 minutes, "**More**" for 45 minutes. Use the "**More**" setting for bone-in meats, like chops, baby back pork ribs or beef short ribs.

BEAN/CHILI – Designed primarily for cooking beans, each mode results in a different bean texture and doneness. For a firmer bean texture, use the **Less** mode; for a softer bean texture, use the **Normal** mode; for a very soft bean texture, use the **More** mode.

POULTRY – How would you like your favorite chicken recipes done in under 40 minutes? You can! Merely adjust for "**Less**" for 5 or minutes, "**More**" for 30 minutes. This can't be beat for preparing a quick batch of shredded chicken for a recipe.

SAUTÉ – Next to "Pressure Cook", this will be your other favorite cooking mode. You can even stir-fry Asian dishes using this mode! Use the **Less** mode for simmering, thickening, reducing liquids and for foods that may burn easily. Use the **Normal** mode for searing. Use the **More** mode for browning and stir-frying. As a safety precaution, this mode times out after 30 minutes.

There are three different sautéing temperature ranges. "**Less**" is primarily used for simmering or thickening a sauce, at a low

275°F to 302°F. "**Normal**" is 320°F to 349°F, excellent for regular sautéing or browning. "**More**" is 347°F to 410°F, perfect for stir-frying or browning.

SLOW COOK – This mode emulates a slow cooker or crockpot. Use the **Less** to correspond to a very low (8 hour) slow cooker setting. Use the **Normal** mode to correspond to a low (6 hour) slow cooker setting. Use the **More** mode to correspond to a high (4 hour) slow cooker setting. The "Slow Cook" button commands three different temperatures: "**Less**" which is 180°F to 190°F(Slow cooker "Warm" setting), "**Normal**" which is 190°F to 200°F(Slow cooker "Low" setting), and "**More**" which is 200°F to 210°F (Slow cooker "High" setting).

RICE – Designed primarily for cooking white rice, this automatic program selects both time and temperature, depending on how much water and rice is in the pot. For rice with a firmer, chewy texture, use the **Less** mode. For rice with a normal texture, use the **Normal** mode. For rice with a softer texture, use the **More** mode. For Basmati, Jasmine, Brown, and Wild rice, use the "**Pressure Cook**" setting instead of "**Rice**".

MULTIGRAIN – This mode is better for brown rice, wild rice, and tougher whole grains. For a firmer texture, use the **Less** mode. For a normal texture, use the **Normal** mode. For a softer texture, use the **More** mode. The **More** setting includes a preset pre-soak period prior to cooking.

PORRIDGE – Use the **Less** mode for Oatmeal; use the **Normal** mode for making rice porridge (congee); use the **More** mode for a porridge / congee that contains a mixture of beans or tougher grains.

STEAM – Programmed specifically for steaming vegetables, it can also be used for other food items. For example, for vegetables alone, use the **Less** mode. For seafood and fish, use the **Normal** mode. For meats, use the **More** mode. Always use the included trivet or a steam pot with feet to elevate food above the water. Use the QR (Quick Release) method to prevent overcooking the food.

YOGURT – The **Less** mode is programmed specifically for Jiu Niang, a sweet fermented rice dish; the **Normal** mode is used to ferment milk when making yogurt, and the **More** mode is for pasteurizing milk.

KEEP WARM – Thee temperatures are available to maintain food at different serving temperatures. All three are approximate temperatures.

Less :133°F, **Normal** :146°F, and **More** :165°F.

Cooking Oil Selection

Selecting a suitable cooking oil depends on how you're going to use it. Each oil has its own "smoke point," the temperature where the oil begins to break down. Always select an oil that has a higher smoke point than whatever temperature you're going to be cooking at. For example, Extra Virgin Olive Oil is not recommended for sautéing. Extra Virgin Olive Oil has a smoke point of 274°F, while sautéing is typically done at temperatures above 320°F. The following table lists cooking oils and their smoke points.

Oil Smoke Points:

Fat	Condition	Smoke Point
Avocado oil	Refined	520°F
Safflower oil	Refined	510°F
Sunflower oil	Neutralized, dewaxed, bleached & deodorized	486–489°F
Butter (Ghee)	Clarified	482°F
Mustard oil		480°F
Bertolli Olive Oil	Extra Light	468°F
Palm oil	Difractionated	455°F
Soybean oil		453°F
Coconut oil	Refined, dry	450°F
Peanut oil	Refined	450°F
Rice bran oil	Refined	450°F
Sesame oil	Semirefined	450°F
Sunflower oil	Semirefined	450°F
Sunflower oil, high oleic	Refined	450°F
Corn oil		446-460°F
Peanut oil		441-445°F
Sunflower oil		441°F
Almond oil		430°F
Canola oil		428°F–446°F
Cottonseed oil	Refined, bleached, deodorized	428–446 °F
Vegetable oil blend	Refined	428°F
Grape seed oil		421°F
Olive oil	Extra Light	410°F

Fat	Condition	Smoke Point
Olive oil	Extra virgin, low acidity, high quality	405°F
Canola oil (Rapeseed)	Refined	400°F
Castor oil	Refined	392°F
Olive oil	Refined	390-470°F
Canola oil (Rapeseed)	Expeller press	375-450°F
Lard		374°F
Olive oil	Extra virgin	374°F
Corn oil	Unrefined	352°F
Coconut oil	Unrefined, dry expeller pressed, virgin	350°F
Sesame oil	Unrefined	350°F
Peanut oil	Unrefined	320°F
Safflower oil	Semirefined	320°F
Sunflower oil, high oleic	Unrefined	320°F
Olive oil	Extra virgin	320°F
Butter		302°F
Canola oil (Rapeseed)	Unrefined	225°F
Flaxseed oil	Unrefined	225°F
Safflower oil	Unrefined	225°F
Sunflower oil	Unrefined, first cold-pressed, raw	225°F

4. Appetizers

Using an Instant Pot® to cook and prepare appetizers is, in the main, overkill. Most of these appetizer recipes use conventional cooking techniques.

4.1. Antipasto Squares

Ingredients:
Cooking spray, for baking sheet
2 cans Pillsbury™ crescent dough sheets
½ lb. deli sliced lechon
¼ lb. thin sliced pepperoni
¼ lb. sliced provolone
¼ lb. sliced mozzarella
1 cup sliced pepperoncini
½ cup sliced black olives
2 tablespoons extra-virgin olive oil
¼ cup grated Parmesan
1 teaspoon dried oregano

Directions:
Preheat oven to 350°F.
Lightly spray a baking sheet with cooking spray.
Unroll a crescent dough sheet onto the sprayed baking sheet.
Layer lechon, mozzarella, pepperoni, provolone, black olives, and pepperoncini.
Leave about a ¼ inch open rim around the sheet.
Unroll a second crescent dough sheet and place on top of the stacked sheet.
Cover with a piece of waxed paper.
Using a rolling pin, lightly press the stack together.
Remove the top waxed paper sheet.
With a wet finger, seal the edges of the stack.
Lightly coat the top sheet with olive oil.
Mix the oregano and Parmesan cheese together and dust the top of the stack.
Bake about 30 minutes, or until dough has turned a rich golden brown.

Use a square of aluminum foil over the dough to prevent burning.
Remove from oven and let rest on a raised wire rack for 15 minutes before cutting.

4.2. Bacon Wrapped Sea Scallop

Ingredients:
10 bacon strips (regular sliced, not thick)
10 sea scallops, cut in half (thickness cut)
20 fresh baby spinach leaves, washed, dried
4 tablespoons butter, divided
1 tablespoon minced garlic
⅓ cup low-sodium chicken broth
Juice of ½ lemon
Plain toothpicks

Directions:
Cut bacon strips in half.
Wrap a spinach leaf around each scallop.
Wrap bacon over spinach and secure with toothpick.
Arrange the wrapped scallops on a baking sheet.
Place a small (⅛ teaspoon) dot of butter on each scallop.
Broil 5 inches from heat for 3 minutes per side, turning until bacon is crisp.
In an 8" deep-sided, non-reactive sauce pan, melt the rest of the butter over medium-high heat.
Add garlic and sauté 1 minute.
Add lemon juice and broth and bring to a boil.
Cook 2 minutes.
Place cooked scallops in a large bowl.
Pour broth over all.
Gently toss scallops to coat. Drain.
Arrange scallops on a serving plate. Poke a toothpick in each.
Reserve liquid as additional dipping sauce.
Makes about 20 appetizers

4.3. Buffalo Pork Ribs

Ingredients:
2 lbs. baby back pork ribs
1 cup water
1 cup Avocado oil
1 teaspoon salt
Toothpicks

Batter Ingredients
1 cup all purpose flour
2 eggs, beaten

Buffalo Sauce Ingredients
½ cup butter
½ cup Piri Piri sauce
2 tablespoons white vinegar
2 teaspoons Worcestershire sauce
¼ teaspoon garlic powder

Directions:
Remove the silverback from the bony side of the ribs.
Place a trivet in the Instant Pot® and wrap the ribs in a circle on the trivet.
Pour in 1 cup of water.
Lock the cover on the Instant Pot® and set the vent lever to "sealing."
Select "Pressure Cook", High Pressure, 45 minutes, "Warm" off.
When the display shows "Off," follow the NPR method and wait 10 minutes.
Follow the QR method to vent residual pressure and steam.
Wait until the pressure indicator pin drops down, then carefully open the lid.

Remove ribs and with a sharp knife, cut the rib meat from the bones.

Dry meat on paper towels. Cut meat into bite-sized pieces. Discard water.

Place the flour in a shallow dish.

Place the eggs in another shallow dish.

Sett the Instant Pot® to "Sauté." When the display shows "Hot", add the oil.

Wait until the display returns to "Hot."

Dredge a piece of rib meat in the eggs, then dredge in the flour.

Fry the coated ribs in the oil until golden brown.

Select "Cancel,"

Drain the cooked ribs on paper towels, spear with toothpicks, and arrange on a serving platter.

Set aside.

In a saucepan melt butter and add Piri Piri, vinegar, Worcestershire, and garlic powder.

Cook over low heat for 2 minutes, stirring occasionally.

Pour sauce into a dipping dish.

Serve with speared ribs.

4.4. Sizzling Tuna Sisig

Ingredients:

8 oz. Ahi tuna steak, boneless, skinless, sliced into small cubes
3 tablespoons Maggi® Liquid Seasoning
3 tablespoons butter, divided
1 medium sweet Vidalia onion, minced
1 – 4 oz. can diced green chiles
4 Thai chiles, stemmed, chopped
2 tablespoons mayonnaise
¼ teaspoon salt
¼ teaspoon freshly ground white pepper
1 teaspoon garlic powder
¼ cup pork chicharon, crushed
½ teaspoon crushed red pepper flakes
1 calamansi, sliced

Directions:

Arrange tuna cubes in a 2 qt. mixing bowl. Mix in liquid seasoning.
Marinate for 15 minutes.
Melt 2 tablespoons butter in a 2 qt. saucepan.
Add the marinated tuna cubes and stir-cook until browned.
Add onion and sauté until translucent.
Add green chiles, Thai chiles, and mayonnaise.
Fold in salt, pepper, and garlic powder.
Stir-cook until all are well blended, about 4 minutes.
Heat a cast iron flat griddle to medium heat on a stovetop burner.
Melt remaining tablespoon butter and coat the entire griddle surface.
Spread the cooked tuna sisig across the heated griddle.
Stir-cook until heated through.

Top with crushed chicharon, red pepper flakes and slices of calamansi.

Serves 4

4.5. Cheesy Crab and Corn Nachos

Ingredients:
1 large bag blue tortilla chips
1 lb. fresh crab meat
1 cup whole kernel corn (canned), drained
1 cup shredded sharp cheddar cheese
4 green onions, thinly sliced
Cheese sauce ingredients:
¼ cup butter
¼ cup all-purpose flour
2 cups whole milk
1 cup shredded sharp cheddar cheese
1 –10 oz. can chopped tomato with green chilies, drained
¼ teaspoon salt
⅛ teaspoon cayenne pepper powder

Directions:
Melt butter in a 1 qt. sauce pan over medium-low heat.
Stir in flour to make a golden roux.
Pour milk in a thin stream into the roux while stirring.
Continue to stir until the texture becomes smooth.
Fold in tomato with chilies, cheese, salt, and cayenne pepper.
Stir until all ingredients are well blended. Set aside.
Preheat oven to 375°F.
Arrange the blue corn tortilla chips on an ovenproof baking
dish. On the chips, alternate layers of crab meat and corn
kernels. Pour the prepared cheese sauce over all.
Sprinkle with more shredded cheese.
Bake for 10 minutes or until the cheese is melted.
Remove dish from oven and sprinkle with green onion.
Serves 6.

4.6. Exquisite Chouriço Beef Nachos

Ingredients:
½ lb. extra lean (85/15) ground beef
½ lb. beef Chouriço, casing removed
1 tablespoon Avocado oil
1 medium yellow onion, chopped
1 tablespoon garlic cloves, minced, divided
1 teaspoon ground cumin, divided
1¾ cups mild salsa verde cruda (recipe in section 8.5)
1 – 15 oz. can black beans, rinsed and drained
½ teaspoon dried Mexican oregano flowers
1 – 4 oz. can diced Ortega™ green chiles, drained
2 Serrano chiles, stemmed, finely chopped
¾ cup water
2 large, ripe avocados
½ teaspoon garlic powder
½ teaspoon onion powder
1 teaspoon lime juice
2 tablespoons chopped fresh cilantro, divided
Coarse Himalayan Pink salt
9 cups restaurant style tortilla chips
2 cups Sargento™ shredded jack cheese
2 cups Sargento™ Mexican Blend shredded cheese

Directions:
Preheat oven to 400°F.
Prepare the Meat:
Set the Instant Pot® to "Sauté." When the display shows "Hot", add the oil.
Stir-cook the beef and Chouriço together until no longer pink. Use a wooden spatula to break up clumps.

Add onion and stir-cook until onion is translucent.

Add the garlic, reserving 1 teaspoon, and stir-cook 30 seconds.

Select the "Cancel" function.

Blend in salsa and the cumin powder, reserving ⅛ teaspoon of the cumin.

Stir-cook, uncovered, until the mixture thickens and all are heated through.

Set aside.

Prepare the Beans:

In a non-reactive saucepan, combine beans, water, green chiles, oregano, and 1 teaspoon garlic.

Bring to a rolling boil, then reduce heat and simmer until the water is almost all evaporated.

Set aside.

Prepare the Guacamole:

Halve and pit the avocados.

Remove the flesh to a mixing bowl.

With a fork, mash together avocados, Serranos, garlic and onion powders, and lime juice.

Add cilantro, salt, and cumin as you may desire.

Set side.

Assemble the Nachos:

On an oven-proof serving dish, arrange a layer of tortilla chips.

Ladle the beans over the chips.

Ladle the meat over the beans.

Dust with the shredded cheeses.

Place dish in oven long enough to melt the cheeses.

Remove from oven and ladle the guacamole over the melted cheese.

Serve with extra chips on the side.

4.7. Exceptional Thai Ground Beef Tacos

Ingredients:
1 lb. extra lean (95/5) ground sirloin
1 cup thinly sliced leek (white part only)
4 cloves garlic, crushed, minced
1 teaspoon red curry paste (recipe in section 8.1)
1 cup Hunt's® tomato sauce
½ cup light coconut milk
1 tablespoon golden brown sugar
1 tablespoon patis (Asian fish sauce)
12 – 6 inch corn tortillas
Grapeseed oil for softening tortillas
Garnishes:
Iceberg lettuce, shredded
Cheddar cheese, shredded
Tomatoes, peeled, seeded, diced
Green onions, thinly sliced
Prepared salsa
Avocado, sliced of mashed

Directions:
Prepare the meat:
Set the Instant Pot® to "Sauté." When the display shows "Hot", add the sirloin.
Stir-cook the sirloin until no longer pink.
Use a wooden spatula to break up clumps.
Stir in the leek and stir-cook until translucent.
Fold in garlic, red curry paste, tomato sauce, patis.
Stir-cook until all are thoroughly mixed.
Blend in coconut milk and sugar.
Bring to a boil, then press "Cancel."

Stir-cook until thickened.

Prepare the tortillas:

In a large, deep sided skillet, pour enough oil to cover a tortilla.

Heat oil to shimmering.

Dredge each tortilla into the hot oil.

When the tortilla begins to bubble, flip it over.

Fold the tortilla into a taco shell and continue to cook until shell becomes slightly stiff.

Remove shell to a paper towel-lined plate and stand the shell, fold up, to drain.

Continue until all 12 shells are made.

Prepare the tacos:

Distribute a heaping tablespoon of the meat mixture into the shell.

Top with a teaspoon of salsa.

Finish with garnishes of your choice.

Serve warm.

4.8. Pork Sisig

Ingredients:

2 lb. pork loin, cut into ¼ inch thick slabs
3 tablespoons low-sodium soy sauce
3 bay leaves
1½ cups water
½ teaspoon salt
1 teaspoon freshly ground white pepper
1 large white onion, finely chopped
2 tablespoons Knorr® seasonings
5 calamansi, juiced
3 roasted Ortega® green chile peppers, chopped.
¼ cup butter
1 large egg, beaten.

Directions:

Place pork in an Instant Pot®, and add soy sauce, garlic, water, and bay leaves.
Cover and lock. Set the vent to "sealing."
Set the Instant Pot® to "Pressure Cook", High pressure, 10 minutes, "Warm" off.
When the display shows "Off," follow the NPR method and wait 10 minutes.
Follow the QR method to vent residual pressure and steam.
Wait until the pressure indicator pin drops down, then carefully open the lid.
Remove pork to a cutting board, pat dry with paper towels, and let cool.
Finely chop the pork.
In a 2 qt. mixing bowl, combine pork, salt, Knorr® seasonings, and onion.
Blend in Ortega® chiles and calamansi juice.
Set the Instant Pot® to "Sauté," "More."

When the display shows "Hot" add the butter.
Add the pork mixture and stir-fry for about 3-5 minutes.
Move the ingredients to the walls.
Add the egg to the center and stir-fry until egg has cooked.
Use a wooden spatula to mix the cooked egg with the rest of the ingredients.
Press the "Cancel" function.
Remove all to a serving bowl.
Serves 6.

4.9. Palitaw

Ingredients:
2 cups of glutinous rice flour
8¾ cup of water, divided
Freshly grated coconut
Sesame seeds, toasted
White powdered sugar

Directions:
Set the Instant Pot® to "Sauté." When the display shows "Hot, add 8 cups of water.
Bring the water to a rolling boil.
Combine the flour and ¾ cup water in a bowl.
Stir until it becomes a smooth dough.
Roll the dough into balls and then flatten each ball.
Drop the flattened balls into the boiling water.
When the rice cakes are ready, they will rise to the surface and float.
Remove the cooked rice cakes and let cool until easily handled.
Select "Cancel."
Roll the rice cakes in freshly grated coconut.
Top cakes with sugar and toasted sesame seeds.
Serve.

4.10. Chouriço and Bell Pepper Tostadas

Ingredients:
1 tablespoon Avocado oil
8 oz. lean ground pork
2 oz. Filipino Chouriço, casing removed
1 large yellow onion, thinly sliced
1 medium red bell pepper, stemmed, cored, seeded, julienned
1 medium yellow bell pepper, stemmed, cored, seeded, julienned
½ teaspoon ground cumin
½ teaspoon dark chili powder
¼ teaspoon Himalayan Pink salt
4 tostada shells
Garnish:
1 ripe avocado, sliced
3 tablespoons crumbled queso fresco
2 tablespoons fresh cilantro leaves
8 lime wedges

Directions:
Set the Instant Pot® to "Saute". When the display shows "Hot", add the oil.
Add pork and chouriço and stir-cook until no longer pink. Use a wooden spatula to break up clumps.
Stir in onion, bell peppers, cumin, chili powder, and salt. Press the "Cancel" function.
Close the lid and lock, setting the vent to "sealing".
Select "Pressure Cook", High Pressure, 4 minutes, "Warm" off.
When the display shows "Off," follow the QR method and release pressure quickly.

Wait until the pressure indicator pin drops down.
Carefully open the lid.
Arrange bell pepper mixture evenly over tostada shells.
Sprinkle each with avocado, queso fresco, and cilantro.
Serve with lime wedges.
Serves 4

5. Main Courses

5.1. Corn on The Cob

Ingredients:
On Trivet:
4 ears fresh corn on the cob (or more, as desired. Do not overcrowd)
1 cup water

In Pot for Butter Flavor:
4 ears fresh corn on the cob (or more, as desired. Do not overcrowd)
1 cup water
½ cup heavy cream, half & half or milk
1 tablespoon white sugar (substitute)
2 tablespoons salted butter

Directions:
On Trivet:
Add water to the Instant Pot® and place the trivet inside.
Lay corn across the trivet. Do not crowd.
Close lid and set pressure valve to "sealing."
Cook on "Steam", High Pressure, for 1 minute.
Perform an NPR and wait for 15 minutes.
Perform a QR to release any residual steam and pressure.
Wait until the pressure indicator pin drops down.
Carefully open the lid and remove corn to a serving platter.
Serve with butter and salt as you may desire.

In Pot for Butter Flavor:
Add all ingredients (corn through butter) to the Instant Pot®.
Close lid and set pressure valve to "sealing."
Cook on "Steam", High Pressure, for 1 minute.
If frozen, cook for 0-1 minute.

Perform an NPR and wait for 15 minutes.

Perform a QR to release any residual steam and pressure.

Wait until the pressure indicator pin drops down.

Carefully open the lid and remove corn to a serving platter.

The longer the corn sits in the liquid, the more flavorful it becomes.

5.2. Beef Steak

Ingredients:
1 lemon, juiced
3 tablespoons soy sauce
1 teaspoon white cane sugar
Himalayan Pink salt and freshly ground white pepper as you may desire
4 lbs. New York strip steak, thinly sliced against the grain
1 tablespoon Tapioca powder
¼ cup Avocado oil
½ cup water
1 medium yellow onion, thinly sliced in rings
2 cloves garlic, crushed, chopped

Directions:
Combine the first 6 ingredients (lemon juice through Tapioca) in a large zipper-topped plastic freezer bag.
Squeeze out the air and seal.
Knead the bag to mix the marinade and to coat the meat.
Refrigerate overnight. Knead occasionally, as you may desire.
Select "Sauté", "More". When the display shows "Hot," add the oil.
Stir-cook the meat until browned all over.
Work in small batches, so as to not crowd the pot.
Remove meat to a serving plate.
Select "Cancel."
Add marinade to Instant Pot®.
Use a wooden spatula to scrape up any brown bits stuck to the bottom of the pot.
Add water, onion, and garlic.
Place a trivet in the Instant Pot® and arrange the meat on it.
Cover and lock the lid. Set vent to "sealing".

Select "Pressure Cook," High Pressure, 6 minutes, "Warm" off.

When the display shows "Off", do an NPR and wait 10 minutes.

QR any remaining pressure and steam.

Wait until the pressure indicator pin drops down.

Carefully open and remove the lid.

With tongs, remove meat to a serving platter.

Remove trivet.

Select "Sauté", "Less" and stir until liquid has thickened.

Select "Cancel."

Pour onions, garlic and cooking liquid over the beef slices and serve.

Serves 4.

5.3. Beef Stir-Fry

Ingredients:
1 lemon, juiced
Himalayan Pink salt and freshly ground white pepper as you may desire
2½ pounds New York strip steak, thinly sliced against the grain
2 tablespoons Tapioca powder
2 tablespoons soy sauce
1½ teaspoon white cane sugar
1 tablespoon Avocado oil
1 lb. snow peas, trimmed
¾ cup green peas
2 stalks celery, sliced
1 red bell pepper, cored, seeded, chopped
1 medium sweet Vidalia onion, thinly sliced in rings
2 cloves garlic, crushed, chopped
1 tablespoon oyster sauce
½ cup water

Directions:
Combine lemon juice, steak, Tapioca powder, soy sauce, and sugar in a large zipper-topped plastic freezer bag.
Squeeze out the air and seal. Knead the bag to mix the marinade and to coat the meat.
Refrigerate at least 1 hour or overnight. Knead occasionally as you may desire.
Turn on the Instant Pot® and select "Sauté", "More."
When the display shows "Hot", add the oil.
Add the beef and sear until browned, 2-3 minutes on each side.
Remove beef to a serving dish.

Add peas, celery, bell pepper, onion, and garlic and stir-cook for a 2-3 minutes.

Press "Cancel" and add beef back in to the Instant Pot®.

Add marinade, oyster sauce and water and stir to mix well.

Close and lock lid. Set valve to "sealing."

Set "Pressure Cook", High pressure, 5 minutes, "Warm" off.

When the display shows "Off", perform the QR method to release remaining pressure and steam.

Wait until the pressure indicator pin drops down.

Carefully open and remove the lid.

Remove beef slices to a serving dish.

Arrange the cooked vegetables around the beef slices and serve.

Serves 4

5.4. Barbecued Beef Brisket

Ingredients:
4 lbs. boneless beef brisket, trimmed
1 cup ketchup
1 cup water
1 tablespoon minced onion
2 tablespoon apple cider vinegar
1 tablespoon bottled white horseradish
1 tablespoon prepared mustard
1 teaspoon Himalayan Pink salt
¼ teaspoon freshly ground white pepper
For serving:
BBQ sauce of your choice

Directions:
In a mixing bowl combine all ingredients except meat.
Place the beef in a large heavy-duty Ziploc® plastic bag.
Pour ketchup mixture over the beef.
Squeeze the air out, seal, and knead to mix marinade and to coat meat.
Cover and refrigerate for several hours, up to overnight.
Pour marinade into the Instant Pot®.
Add the meat, fat side up.
Close and lock the lid. Set the vent to "sealing."
Select "Pressure Cook", High pressure, 60 minutes, "Warm" off.
When the display shows "Off", let the pressure release naturally for 15 minutes.
Perform the QR method to release any remaining pressure and steam.
Wait until the pressure indicator pin drops down.
Carefully open and remove the lid.

Carefully remove the meat to a large platter and slice meat across the grain.
Serve with BBQ sauce mixed with some of the cooking liquid.
Serves 8

Note: slice the brisket in half to fit inside the Instant Pot®.

5.5. Roast Beef Tenderloin with Veggies

Ingredients:
For the Tenderloin:

3 ½ lb. beef tenderloin roast, trimmed

1 teaspoon garlic powder

1 teaspoon dry mustard powder

¾ tablespoon black pepper

2 cloves garlic, crushed, minced

1 small red onion, sliced into rings

1 cup water

For the vegetables:

3 large carrots, peeled and chopped into ½ inch lengths

3 large red, new potatoes, skin on and quartered

1 teaspoon Himalayan Pink salt

1 teaspoon onion powder

1 teaspoon freshly ground white pepper

1 teaspoon Avocado oil

Directions:
To Prepare the Tenderloin:

In a small mixing bowl, combine garlic powder, mustard powder, pepper, and garlic.

Rub meat all over with mixture.

Place a trivet in the Instant Pot®. Add water.

Place meat on trivet and top with onion slices.

Close and lock the lid. Set the vent to "sealing."

Select "Pressure Cook", High pressure, 50 minutes, "Warm" off.

When the display shows "Off", use the NPR method and wait 15 minutes.

Perform the QR method to release any residual pressure and steam.

Wait until the pressure indicator pin drops down.

Carefully open and remove the lid.

Remove tenderloin to a serving plate and cover with aluminum foil.

Let rest about 10 minutes before slicing.

To Prepare the Vegetables:

In a 3 qt. mixing bowl, combine the vegetables, oil, salt and pepper.

Toss to coat thoroughly.

Place coated vegetables in a footed steamer basket and place in the Instant Pot®.

Close and seal lid, setting the vent to "sealing."

Select "Pressure Cook", High pressure, 10 minutes, "Warm" off.

When the display shows "Off", perform the QR method to release any residual pressure and steam.

When pressure indicator pin drops, carefully remove lid.

Remove the vegetables to a serving bowl.

5.6. Palawan Special Beef

Ingredients:
2 tablespoons Grapeseed oil
1 lb. boneless beef sirloin, cut into thin, two-inch long strips
¼ teaspoon crushed red pepper flakes
3 green onions, chopped
6 cloves garlic, crushed, minced
1 teaspoon ground cumin
½ teaspoon salt as you may desire
½ teaspoon golden brown sugar
6 stalks Bok Choy, washed and cut into two-inch lengths
¼ cup Bok Choy leaves, coarsely minced

Directions:
Set the Instant Pot® to "Sauté", "More". When the display shows "Hot," add the oil.
Add beef and stir-fry about one minute.
Drain meat and set aside.
Add pepper flakes, green onions, garlic, and cumin and stir-fry for 1 minute.
Add the Bok Choy and stir-fry for two minutes.
Return the beef to the Instant Pot® and stir-fry 1 minute.
Add salt, sugar, and the Bok Choy.
Stir-fry 30 seconds, tossing to coat.
Press "Cancel" and remove all to a serving platter.
Serves 4.

5.7. Beef Tapsilog

Ingredients:
For Tapa:
1 lb. beef sirloin, thinly sliced into ½ inch strips
½ teaspoon garlic powder
2 tablespoons golden brown sugar
1 tablespoon low sodium soy sauce
¼ cup apple cider vinegar
1 teaspoon Himalayan Pink salt, or as you may desire
1 teaspoon freshly ground white pepper, or as you may desire
4 tablespoons Avocado oil, divided
For Garlic Fried Rice and Egg:
1 cup cooked Basmati rice
¼ teaspoon garlic powder
1 teaspoon salt, or as you may desire
1 egg, fried sunny side up

Directions:
In a zipper-topped plastic bag, combine beef, garlic, sugar, and soy sauce.
Add vinegar, salt, and pepper.
Squeeze out all the air and seal.
Knead to mix and to coat the meat with marinade.
Refrigerate overnight.
Set the Instant Pot® to "Sauté", "More". When the display shows "Hot", add 2 tablespoons oil.
Stir in the rice, using a wooden spatula to break up clumps.
Dust with the garlic powder and salt.
Stir-fry until rice is mixed and heated through.
Remove rice to a serving dish.
Add the remaining oil and heat over medium to low heat.
Stir-fry beef and marinade until cooked as you like it.
Press the "Cancel" function.

Remove the beef and drain on paper towels.
Arrange the cooked beef on the bed of rice.
Top with the fried egg.
Serve.

5.8. Beef Nilaga

Ingredients:
4 lb. beef bone-in short ribs
2 medium onions, diced
2 large potatoes, chunked in bite-sized pieces
2 medium carrots, cut on the bias into bite-sized pieces
1 medium head cabbage, cut into quarters.
1 quart water
Sea Salt as you may desire
Freshly ground black pepper as you may desire
Sriracha Hot Sauce

Directions:
In the Instant Pot, put in short ribs and enough water to cover.
Close and seal lid, setting the vent to "sealing."
Select "Stew", High pressure, 15 minutes, "Warm" off.
When display shows "Off", QR the pressure.
When pressure indicator pin drops, carefully remove lid.
Remove ribs to a serving platter.
Pour out and discard water.
Add 1 quart water to the Instant Pot.
Add ribs, onions, carrots, potatoes, and Sriracha.
Close and seal lid, setting the vent to "sealing"
Select "Pressure Cook", High pressure, 45 minutes, "Warm" off.
When display shows "Off", perform an NPR and wait 10 minutes.
QR the residual pressure and steam.
When pressure indicator pin drops, carefully remove lid.
Remove all to a serving platter, reserving liquid in the pot.
Season meat and vegetables as you may desire.
Press "Warm" function.
Add cabbage and cook until cabbage is done, about 5 minutes

Press "Cancel."
Remove cabbage to the serving platter.
Serves 4

5.9. Signature Adobo Chicken

Ingredients:
4 chicken legs, thighs and drumsticks separated
Kosher salt and freshly ground black pepper
2 tablespoons Avocado oil
⅓ cup low sodium soy sauce
¼ cup sugar
¼ cup white distilled vinegar
½ cup water
5 cloves garlic, smashed
2 bay leaves
1 large yellow onion, sliced
2 scallions, thinly sliced, for serving
Cooked long grain rice, for serving

Directions:
Season the chicken legs generously with salt and pepper.
Set the Instant Pot® to "Sauté". When the display shows "Hot", add the oil.
Add half the chicken pieces and brown on both sides, about 7 minutes.
Remove with tongs to a plate and brown the remaining chicken pieces.
Return all the chicken to the Instant Pot®.
Add the soy sauce, sugar, vinegar, garlic, bay leaves, onion and ½ teaspoon pepper.
Close and seal lid, setting the vent to "sealing."
Select "Pressure Cook", High pressure, 8 minutes, "Warm" off.
When display shows "Off", perform the QR method to release the pressure and steam.
When pressure indicator pin drops, carefully remove lid.
Set the Instant Pot® to "Sauté".
Let the sauce come to a boil and reduce it until dark brown and very fragrant, about 20 minutes. Remove the bay leaves.
Transfer the chicken and sauce to a serving platter, sprinkle with scallions and serve with rice.

5.10. Chicken Afritada

Ingredients:
¼ cup grapeseed oil
2 lb. boneless, skinless chicken, cut into bite-sized pieces
3 cloves garlic, chopped
1 small yellow onion, sliced
2 large tomatoes, finely chopped
8 oz. can Contadina® tomato sauce
1 cup water
Sriracha hot chili sauce
1 teaspoon white sugar
1 medium orange sweet potato, peeled, cubed
1 carrot, cut into cubes
1 red bell pepper, cored, seeded, sliced
1 green bell pepper, cored, seeded, sliced
½ cup green peas (optional)
garlic salt and freshly ground white pepper as you may desire

Directions:
Set the Instant Pot® to "Sauté". When the display shows "Hot", add the oil.
Add the chicken, onion, garlic and sauté until chicken is no longer pink.
Press "Cancel."
Add tomatoes, tomato sauce, water, salt and pepper, and sugar and stir to mix well.
Close and seal lid, setting the vent to "sealing".
Select "Pressure Cook", High pressure, 15 minutes, "Warm" off.
When display shows "Off", perform the NPR method and wait 10 minutes.
Perform the QR method to release pressure and steam.
When pressure indicator pin drops, carefully remove lid.
Add the potato, carrot, bell peppers, Sriracha, and peas.
Close and seal lid, setting the vent to "sealing".

Select "Warm", low pressure, 10 minutes.
At the end of 10 minutes, perform the QR method to release pressure and steam.
When pressure indicator pin drops, carefully remove lid.
Serves 4

5.11. Pinoy Pork Ribs

Ingredients:
4 tablespoons Avocado oil, divided
1 rack of Pork bone-in baby back ribs
4 garlic cloves, crushed
1 medium yellow onion, sliced
1 cup low-sodium soy sauce
1 cup water
1 cup Mafran® Banana sauce
½ cup golden brown sugar
3 tablespoons lemon juice
BBQ sauce (recipe follows)
Basmati rice, cooked, for serving

Directions:
Remove the silverback from the bony side of the ribs.
Use a butter knife to loosen, and then use a paper towel to grab and strip off the silverback.
Cut the rack of ribs into three sections of about 4 bones each.
Select "Sauté" function. When the display shows "Hot," add 3 tablespoons oil.
Sauté the ribs, one section at a time and remove them to a serving platter.
Add remaining oil, if necessary.
Add the garlic and onions and sauté.
Once the onions are translucent, press the "Cancel" button.
In a small mixing bowl, blend together the soy sauce, water, Mafran®, sugar, and lemon juice.
Mix until well blended and then pour into the Instant Pot®.
Using a wooden spatula, scrape up the burned meaty bits.
Add the ribs back in to the Instant Pot®, and submerge them in the cooking liquid.
Make sure the meat is submerged in the liquid. Add a little more water just to cover ribs.
Close and seal lid, setting the vent to "sealing".

Select "Pressure Cook", High pressure, 45 minutes, "Warm" off.
When the display shows "Off", perform the NPR method and wait 10 minutes.
Perform the QR method to release residual pressure and steam.
When pressure indicator pin drops, carefully remove lid.
SKIP THESE NEXT STEPS if you don't want crispy ribs.
Preheat your oven to "Broil."
Remove the ribs and place them on a foil lined baking sheet.
Baste them with BBQ sauce and some of the liquid from the Instant Pot®.
Place them in the oven, meat side up, and broil until they are as crispy as you may desire.
Serve with long grain Basmati rice.

BBQ sauce
Ingredients:
1 cup rice vinegar
1 tablespoon low-sodium soy sauce
2 tablespoons light brown sugar
2 tablespoons banana ketchup
1 teaspoon crushed red pepper flakes
1 tablespoon bourbon
2 teaspoons fish sauce
¼ teaspoon Chinese 5 spice powder
1 teaspoon salt
1 teaspoon black pepper
Juice and zest of 1 lime

Directions:
Combine all ingredients in a saucepan over medium-low heat.
Stir-cook until sugar is dissolved.
Let cool and store in a wide mouthed jar.

5.12. Filipino Breakfast Frittata

Ingredients:
2 – 6 inch corn tortillas
2 tablespoons butter
2 tablespoons longganiza sausage, cooked, crumbled
1 habanero pepper, cored, seeded, minced
2 garlic cloves, crushed, minced
1 green onion, thinly sliced
2 large eggs, beaten
Mild Pace™ picante salsa, for serving.

Directions:
Set the Instant Pot® to "Sauté", "Less" function. When display shows "Hot," add butter.
Soften the tortillas in the melted butter. Remove to a serving plate.
Add the sausage, habanero, green onions and garlic and stir-cook until fragrant.
Mound the vegetables and pour the eggs over them.
Let set a bit then place a tortilla over the egg mixture.
Gently press down on the tortilla to incorporate it with the eggs.
Let cook a bit to begin to set the eggs then flip the omelet.
Wrap any egg that extends out from the under the tortilla.
Cover with the second tortilla and cook until the eggs are set.
Remove frittata to a plate and spread some salsa over the tortilla.
Select "Cancel."
Serve while hot.
Serves 1

5.13. Pork Binagoongan

Ingredients:
4 cups water
2 pounds pork liempo, cut in 1 inch cubes
1 tablespoon Avocado oil
½ cup shrimp bagoong
4 cloves garlic; minced
1 small yellow onion, chopped
1 medium tomato, peeled, cored, cut into eight pieces
1 teaspoon Philippine bird's eye peppers (siling labuyo)
5 tablespoon white vinegar
½ tablespoon golden brown sugar
1 green bell pepper, stemmed, cored, seeded, diced
1 eggplant, cubed
Basmati rice, cooked, for serving

Directions:
Add 4 cups water to your Instant Pot®.
Add pork.
Close and lock the lid. Set the vent to "sealing."
Select "Pressure Cook," High pressure, 15 minutes, "Warm" off.
When the display shows "Off," perform the QR method to release pressure and steam.
Wait until the pressure indicator pin drops down.
Carefully open and remove the lid.
Drain pork and place in a serving bowl. return to the Instant Pot®.
Select "Sauté". When the display shows "Hot," add oil.
Sauté garlic, onion, and tomato until onion is translucent.
Crush the tomato with a wooden spoon.
Add pork and shrimp bagoong. Stir-cook to combine and heat through.

Add vinegar and siling labuyo. Stir-cook to combine and heat through.

Add sugar, eggplant, and bell peppers.

Continue stir-cooking until the eggplant and bell peppers are softened.

Press "Cancel" and remove all to a serving bowl.

Serve with cooked Basmati rice.

Serves 6

5.14. Spicy Grilled Prawns

Ingredients:
1 large clove garlic, crushed, minced
1 tablespoon Kosher salt
⅛ teaspoon hot Hungarian paprika (or cayenne pepper)
1 teaspoon sweet Hungarian paprika
2 tablespoons virgin olive oil
2 teaspoons lemon juice
2 tablespoons Avocado oil
2 pounds large shrimp, peeled and deveined
8 wedges lemon, for garnish

Directions:
Select "Sauté". When the Instant Pot® display shows "Hot," add the oil
In a large bowl, combine the first six (garlic through lemon) ingredients to form a paste.
Toss shrimp with paste until evenly coated.
Stir-cook shrimp for 2 to 3 minutes per side, or until opaque. Select "Cancel."
Remove shrimp to a suitable plate. Garnish with lemon wedges.
Serves 8

5.15. Kare-Kare

Ingredients:
1 lb. beef stew meat (or oxtail)
2 tablespoons Avocado oil
1 eggplant, sliced into ¼ inch sections
water
1 cup Chinese long beans, cut in 2 inch-long pieces
3-4 whole baby bok choy, washed
1 teaspoon baking soda
1 cup peanut butter (creamy or chunky)
3 cups low sodium chicken broth, divided
1 beef bouillon cube
1 tablespoon fish sauce
1 tablespoon annatto powder (optional)
1 medium yellow onion, sliced in wedges
4 cloves garlic, chopped
1 cup ground toasted rice
½ cup ground nuts
shrimp paste
salt and freshly ground black pepper as you may desire

Cooked Basmati rice, for serving

Directions:
Select "Sauté". When the display shows "Hot," add 1 tablespoon oil.
When the oil is shimmering, add the meat and stir-cook to brown.
Remove the browned meat to a bowl and set aside.
Put in the onions and sauté them until onions are translucent.
Add, garlic, bouillon cube, fish sauce, and 1 cup chicken broth.
Using a wooden spatula, scrape up all stuck pieces from the bottom of the pot.

Add the rest of the broth and the browned meat.

Bring to a boil. Press "Cancel." Close and seal the lid. Set the vent to "sealing."

Select "Pressure Cook", High pressure, 30 minutes (45 minutes for oxtail).

When the display shows "Off", use the QR method to release pressure and steam.

Wait until the pressure indicator pin drops down and then carefully remove the lid.

Remove meat to a serving bowl and set aside.

Fry the eggplant in a skillet with the remaining oil.

Bring a medium saucepan of water to boiling. Stir in baking soda.

Add bok choy and long beans and blanch not longer than 2 minutes.

Using a wire strainer, drain and remove vegetables to another serving bowl.

Add the peanut butter, annatto powder, ground rice, and nuts to the vegetables.

Using a whisk, stir well. Adjust the seasonings by adding salt and pepper.

Fold the meat back into the vegetables. Stir to combine and coat the meat.

Remove to individual serving bowls. Top with shrimp paste as you may desire.

Serve with lots of rice!

5.16. Kikiam

Ingredients:
1 lb. ground pork
½ lb. shrimp, minced
1 medium carrot, minced
1 medium red onion, minced
1 tablespoon five spice powder
2 teaspoons salt as you may desire
½ teaspoon freshly ground white pepper
1 tablespoon Tapioca powder dissolved in 2 tablespoons water
6 pieces bean curd sheets (tawpe)
1 cup water
3 cups cooking oil
Sweet chili sauce for dipping

Directions:
In a large mixing bowl, combine the first seven (pork through pepper) ingredients.
Mix well.
Lay a piece of bean curd sheet flat on a table.
Place a generous scoop of the meat mixture in the center.
Fold and roll like a large spring roll.
Seal the end by dipping your finger in the Tapioca mixture and wetting the inside edge.
Alternatively, wrap with a piece of butcher's string and tie of end.
Pour 1 cup of water into the Instant Pot®.
Arrange the kikiam in the steamer basket.
Close and seal lid, setting the vent to "sealing".
Select "Steam", High pressure, 15 minutes, "Warm" off.
When the display shows "Off", perform the QR method to release all pressure and steam.

Wait until the pressure indicator pin drops down.
Carefully open and remove the lid.
Remove the kikiam from the steamer and then set aside.
Heat the cooking oil in a 5 qt. Dutch oven.
Deep fry the kikiam until the wrapper turns golden brown.
Remove from the pan and then slice into serving pieces.
Serve with sweet chili sauce.
Makes 6 pieces.

5.17. Arroz Caldo

Ingredients:
1 tablespoon ghee or extra light olive oil
1 medium yellow onion, chopped
1 thumb size ginger, peeled, julienned
3 chicken thighs, boneless, skinless, cut in half to make 6 pieces.
½ cup uncooked rice
4 cups water
Juice of ½ lemon
1½ tablespoon fish sauce
1 teaspoon salt
1 teaspoon freshly ground white pepper
chopped green onion or roasted garlic chips as topping optional

Directions:
Select "Sauté".
When the Instant Pot® display shows "Hot," add the oil.
Add onion and ginger and sauté for about 2 minutes.
Add chicken and sauté for one minute on each side.
Select "Cancel."
Stir in water, rice, lemon juice, fish sauce, salt and pepper.
Seal cover on your Instant Pot®, making sure vent is in the sealed position.
Press "SOUP", "Normal setting", 25 minutes, "Warm" off.
When the display shows "Off", perform the NPR method and wait 10 minutes.
Follow the QR method to release any residual pressure and steam. Wait until the pressure indicator pin drops down.
Carefully open and remove the lid.
Skim and discard about ½ cup of oil/liquid from the top of the arroz caldo.
Remove soup to a serving bowl and enjoy!

5.18. Beef Asado

Ingredients:
½ lb. beef, thinly sliced
¼ cup low sodium soy sauce
1 tablespoon calamansi juice
1 cup water, divided
2 tablespoons Avocado oil
1 large yellow onion, cut into rings
1 tablespoon Avocado oil

Directions:
Place beef in a plastic bag.
Add soy sauce, calamansi and ½ cup water.
Squeeze the air out, seal, and knead to coat meat.
Marinate for an hour in the refrigerator.
Select "Sauté." When the display shows "Hot", add the oil.
Add onions, and beef.
Sauté for about 3-5 minutes until meat is lightly browned.
Select "Cancel."
Add the marinade and the remaining water.
Close and seal lid, setting the vent to "sealing".
Select "Pressure Cook", High pressure, 15 minutes, "Warm" off.
At the multiple beeps, perform the NPR method and wait 10 minutes
Perform the QR method to release remaining pressure and steam.
When pressure indicator pin drops, carefully remove lid.
Remove all to a serving plate.
Serve hot.

5.19. Pork Afritada

Ingredients:
1½ lb. ground pork
1 large Yukon potato, cut into wedges
1 large carrot, cut into wedges
3 bay leaves
1– 15 oz. can Contadina® tomato sauce
1 teaspoon freshly ground white pepper
8 oz. low-sodium beef broth
½ cup water
1 small red bell pepper, cored, seeded, julienned
1 small green bell pepper, cored, seeded, julienned
1 garlic clove, crushed, minced
1 medium yellow onion, chopped
2 tablespoons Avocado oil
Himalayan Pink Salt and freshly ground black pepper as you may desire
Cooked Basmati rice, for serving

Directions:
Select "Sauté," "More." When the display shows "Hot", add the oil.
Sauté onions until translucent.
Add the pork and sauté until no longer pink.
Add the garlic and stir-fry 1 minute.
Select "Cancel."
Add the bay leaves, beef broth, water, and tomato sauce.
Add the potato, bell peppers and carrots. Stir to blend.
Close and lock lid. Set the vent to "sealing".
Select "Pressure Cook," High pressure, 15 minutes, "Warm" off.
When the display shows "Off," perform the NPR method and wait 10 minutes
Perform the QR method to release remaining pressure and steam.

Wait until the pressure indicator pin drops down.
Carefully open and remove the lid.
Remove all to a serving bowl.
Adjust seasonings as you may desire.
Serve with cooked Basmati rice.
Serves 6

5.20. Togue Guisado (Sautéed Bean Sprouts with Pork)

Ingredients:
½ lb. pork, thinly sliced
1 tablespoon Avocado oil
5 cloves garlic, minced
1 medium yellow onion, diced
1 carrot, julienned
1 red bell pepper, cored, seeded, julienned
1 green bell pepper, cored, seeded, julienned
2 tablespoons low-sodium soy sauce
2 tablespoons Japanese Goyoza sauce (optional)
Himalayan Pink salt and freshly ground black pepper as you may desire
12 oz. *togue* (bean sprouts)
½ cup low-sodium chicken broth
1 tablespoon Tapioca powder dissolved in 2 tablespoons water.
3 green onions, thinly sliced, for garnishing

Directions:
Select "Sauté," "More." When the display shows "Hot," add the oil.
Add the pork and sauté until no longer pink.
Add onions and sauté until translucent.
Add carrots and bell peppers and stir-fry 3 minutes.
Add the garlic and stir-fry 1 minute.
Select "Cancel."
Season with soy sauce, Goyoza sauce (if using), salt and pepper.
Add broth and *togue* (bean sprouts).
Close and lock the lid. Set the vent to "sealing."

Select "Pressure Cook," High pressure, 8 minutes, "Warm" off.

When the display shows "Off," perform the NPR method and wait 10 minutes.

Follow the QR method to release any residual pressure and steam.

Wait until the pressure indicator pin drops down.

Carefully open and remove the lid.

Add the dissolved Tapioca powder to the Instant Pot®'s liquid.

Stir to thicken and toss all to coat.

Garnish with sliced green onions and remove contents to a serving bowl.

Serves 6

5.21. Giniling Guisado (Ground Beef with Bell Peppers)

Ingredients:
1 lb. lean (80/20) ground beef
1 medium yellow onion, diced
1 large Yukon potato, peeled, cut into bite-sized pieces
4 medium Roma tomatoes, diced
1 medium green bell pepper, cored, seeded, diced
1 medium red bell pepper, cored, seeded, diced
4 cloves of garlic, crushed, minced
3 tablespoons low-sodium soy sauce
2 tablespoons Sweet Hungarian Paprika
1 teaspoon hot Hungarian Paprika.
1 tablespoon raisins
1 teaspoon freshly ground black pepper
1 cup water
Garlic salt to taste
For serving:
Mezzetti® Hot Chili Peppers for spiciness
Cooked Basmati rice

Directions:
Select "Sauté." When the display shows "Hot," add the ground beef.
Stir-cook meat until no longer pink.
Use a wooden spatula to break up clumps and to scrape up any burned bits.
Add onion and sauté until translucent.
Stir in the garlic, tomato, soy sauce, both Paprikas, and bell peppers.
Stir-cook until Paprikas are fragrant.
Select "Cancel."

Add potatoes, raisins, and water.

Close and lock the lid. Set the vent to "sealing."

Select "Pressure Cook," High pressure, 15 minutes, "Warm" off.

When the display shows "Off," perform the NPR method and wait 10 minutes.

Follow the QR method to release any residual pressure and steam.

Wait until the pressure indicator pin drops down.

Carefully open and remove the lid.

Add salt and pepper as you may desire.

Serve with rice and thinly sliced hot chili peppers.

Serves 4

5.22. Sweet Beef Short Ribs

Ingredients:
2 lbs. beef short ribs
1 cup low-sodium soy sauce
1 cup water
¼ cup sesame oil
4 green onions, thinly sliced
2 cloves garlic, minced
½ cup white cane sugar
2 tablespoons toasted sesame seeds
1 teaspoon freshly ground white pepper
¼ cup Avocado oil

Directions:
Wash the short ribs to remove any bone chips.
With the tip of a sharp knife, make small slits in the meaty portion, cutting almost to the bone.
In a gallon zipper-topped plastic freezer bag, combine all ingredients (ribs through pepper) except Avocado oil.
Squeeze out the air and seal the bag.
Knead the bag to mix the marinade and to thoroughly coat the meat.
Refrigerate the meat overnight. Knead again at least once.
Select "Sauté." When the display shows "Hot," add the oil.
Brown the ribs all over in small batches, but do not crowd.
Remove ribs to a serving plate.
Select "Cancel."
Add marinade to the Instant Pot®.
Use a wooden spatula to scrape up any brown bits stuck to the bottom of the pot.
Stand ribs on edge.
Close and lock lid. Set vent to "sealing."

Select "Pressure Cook", High Pressure, "Warm" off, 45 minutes cook time*.

When the display shows "Off," perform the NPR method and wait 10 minutes.

Follow the QR method to release any residual pressure and steam.

Wait until the pressure indicator pin drops down.

Carefully open and remove the lid.

With tongs, remove ribs to a serving platter and let rest 5 minutes.

Serves 4.

Note: *After 45 minutes cook time - check the ribs for tenderness and if necessary, "Pressure Cook" ribs 15 more minutes until the meat is fall-off-the-bone tender.

5.23. Beef Caldereta (Kalderetang Baka)

Ingredients:
2 tablespoons Avocado oil
1 large Yukon potato, peeled, cubed
1 cup carrots, bias-cut into 1 inch pieces
1 large green bell pepper, cored, seeded, cubed
1 lb. beef stew meat, cut into 2 inch cubes
5 cloves garlic, chopped
1 large yellow onion, chopped
4 Roma tomatoes, peeled, seeded, chopped
1 cup low-sodium beef broth
1 beef bouillon cube
salt and pepper as you may desire
1– 10 oz. can coconut milk
¼ cup liver spread
4-6 tablespoons low-sodium tomato paste
¼ cup green peas

Directions:
Select "Sauté." When the display shows "Hot," add the oil.
Sauté potatoes, carrots and bell pepper until vegetables are softened. Set aside.
Add beef and sauté, tossing to brown on all sides.
Add garlic, onions, and tomato. Sauté until onions are translucent.
Select "Cancel."
Add broth and bouillon. Salt and pepper as you may desire
Using a wooden spatula, scrape up any burned bits.
Close and lock lid. Set the vent to "sealing."
Select "Pressure Cook", High pressure, 35 minutes, "Warm" off.

At the beep, follow the NPR method and wait 5 minutes.
Follow the QR method and release any residual pressure and steam.
Carefully open the lid.
Select "Sauté" and add the coconut milk and tomato paste.
Let it boil uncovered until it thickens.
Add the liver spread. Stir-cook until thickened.
Put in the cooked vegetables and the green peas.
Select "Cancel."
Stir in the cooked beef.
Serve with cups of rice!

6. Soups and Side Dishes

6.1. Pork and Noodle

Ingredients:
2 tablespoons Avocado oil
½ lb. ground pork
½ large yellow onion, diced
2 garlic cloves, crushed, minced
4 cups low-sodium chicken broth
¼ lb. angel hair pasta noodles
1 egg, lightly beaten
1 tablespoon low-sodium soy sauce
2 teaspoons fresh ground pepper
For serving:
fresh cilantro, chopped
lime, wedges

Directions:
Select "Sauté." When the display shows "Hot," add the oil.
Add pork and sauté until no longer pink.
Use a wooden spatula to break up clumps and to scrape up any burned bits.
Add onion and sauté until translucent.
Add garlic and sauté 30 seconds.
Add broth and pepper and bring to a boil.
Add noodles and simmer 3 minutes or until noodles are done.
When noodles are ready, add soy sauce and egg.
Allow to thicken slightly and ladle into individual bowls.
Select "Cancel."
Garnish with cilantro and fresh squeezed lime.
Serves 4

6.2. Broccoli and Beef Short Ribs

Ingredients:
2 lbs. beef short ribs
1 large onion, sliced
2 cups water
2 medium sized tomatoes, quartered
1 medium head broccoli, washed, loosely chopped.
2 pack sinigang mix
3 miniature hot banana peppers

Directions:
Wash the meat to remove excess fat and any bone chips.
Place meat in the Instant Pot®. Add water, chopped onions, tomatoes, sinigang mix packet, fresh peppers.
Close and lock the lid. Set the vent to "sealing."
Select "Pressure Cook," High pressure, 45 minutes, "Warm" off. When the display shows "Off," perform the NPR method and wait 10 minutes.
Follow the QR method to release any residual pressure and steam. Wait until the pressure indicator pin drops down.
Carefully open and remove the lid.
Add another packet of sinigang mix.
Add broccoli and close and seal lid, setting the vent to "sealing."
Select "Pressure Cook", High pressure, 0 minutes, "Warm" off.
When the display shows "Off," perform the QR method to release pressure and steam.
Wait until the pressure indicator pin drops down.
Carefully open and remove the lid.
Serve.

Tip: Use pork or chicken instead of beef. Combine pork, beef, chicken as a pleasant variation.

6.3. Soul-Warming Lomi Noodle Soup

Ingredients:
12 oz. wide egg noodles
¼ cup diced Chouriço caseless sausage
2 cups low-sodium chicken broth
2 large eggs, lightly beaten
¾ teaspoon garlic powder
½ small yellow onion, thinly sliced
1 tablespoon diced red bell pepper, cored, seeded
4 green onions, thinly sliced
4 oz. Napa cabbage, roughly chopped
2 tablespoons butter
1 teaspoon low sodium soy sauce
1 teaspoon freshly ground white pepper
1 tablespoon Tapioca powder dissolved in 2 tablespoons water

Directions:
Select "Sauté," "More." When the display shows "Hot," add and melt butter. Stir-cook yellow onion until lightly caramelized. Add bell pepper and sauté until softened.
Fold in Chouriço and stir-cook until browned. Use a wooden spatula to break up clumps.
Add the broth, dry spices, soy sauce and pepper and bring to a rolling boil. While stirring, drizzle in the beaten eggs to make egg threads. Fold in the noodles and boil until noodles are al dente. Stir in cabbage and cook until cabbage is wilted. Fold in green onions. Stir-cook 2 minutes.
Add dissolved Tapioca powder and stir until thickened. Select "Cancel."
Serves 4.

6.4. Basmati Rice

Ingredients:
2 cups long grain Basmati rice
2 ½ cups water

Directions:
Place rice in a fine-mesh strainer and rinse under cold water. Drain well.

Pour the water into your Instant Pot®. Add the rice and swirl to combine.

Make sure that all of the rice is in the water and that no grains of rice are on the sides of the Instant Pot®.

Close and lock the lid. Set the vent to "sealing."

Select "Pressure Cook," High pressure, 4 minutes, "Warm" off.

When the display shows "Off," perform the NPR method and wait 10 minutes.

Follow the QR method to release any residual pressure and steam.

Wait until the pressure indicator pin drops down.

Carefully open and remove the lid.

Fluff rice and serve.

6.5. Macaroni Soup (Sopas)

Ingredients:
2 tablespoons Avocado oil
1 tablespoon unsalted butter
1 medium yellow onion, sliced
3 cloves garlic, crushed
3 cups water, divided
2 chicken thighs (skinless, bone-in)
Himalayan Pink salt and freshly ground white pepper as you may desire
1 carrot, diced
2 cups uncooked elbow macaroni (or shell macaroni)
3 Vienna sausages, thinly sliced
¼ lb. Napa cabbage, thinly sliced
1 cup whole milk
4 green onions, chopped, for garnish

Directions:
Select "Sauté." When the display shows "Hot," add oil and melt butter.
Sauté onions until translucent.
Add garlic and sauté 30 seconds.
Select "Cancel" and let Instant Pot® cool until you can handle it.
Add 1 cup water and chicken.
Close and lock the lid. Set the vent to "sealing."
Select "Pressure Cook," High pressure, 10 minutes, "Warm" off.
When the display shows "Off," perform the NPR method and wait 10 minutes.
Follow the QR method to release any residual pressure and steam.
Wait until the pressure indicator pin drops down.

Carefully open and remove the lid.

Remove chicken to a plate and let cool.

Shred the cooked chicken meat with two forks, and discard the bones.

Add macaroni and enough water to just cover macaroni.

Close and lock the lid. Set the vent to "sealing."

Select "Pressure Cook", HIGH pressure for [half the time that is recommended on the box].

Select "Warm" off.

When the display shows "Off," follow the QR method to vent residual pressure and steam.

Wait until the pressure indicator pin drops down.

Carefully open and remove lid.

Put shredded chicken back into the pot.

Add carrots and sausages.

Select "Warm," and simmer until carrots are fork-tender.

Fold in cabbage and milk and simmer for another 5 more minutes.

Serve into individual bowls and garnish with green onions.
Serves 4 to 6.

6.6. Pork Sinigang

Ingredients:
1 enormous yellow onion, chopped
2 plump Beefsteak tomatoes, cut into ½ inch dice
1 lb. pork chops, bone-in
1 cup water, more if needed
1 – 1.41 oz. package tamarind soup base
½ lb. cut broccoli*
Yellow peppers (optional)

Directions:
Wash meat three times
Put water, meat, tomatoes, and onions in the Instant Pot®.
Add one packet of Knorr® tamarind soup base.
Close and lock the lid. Set the vent to "sealing."
Select "Pressure Cook," High pressure, 14 minutes, "Warm" off.
When the display shows "Off," perform the NPR method and wait 10 minutes.
Follow the QR method to release any residual pressure and steam.
Wait until the pressure indicator pin drops down.
Carefully open and remove the lid.
Stir in the broccoli*.
Select "Warm" and simmer until the broccoli is tender
Don't overcook the broccoli.
Add yellow peppers if you like your sinigang spicy.

* broccoli - you can put broccoli by itself or Kangkong leaves, radish, taro, green beans.

6.7. Callos

Ingredients:
3-4 lb. beef short ribs
1–15 oz. can garbanzo beans
1– 8 oz. can tomato sauce
2 pieces chorizo de bilbao, sliced
¼ lb. bacon, sliced crosswise in 1 inch length
1 large red bell pepper, cored, seeded, cut into thick strips lengthwise
1 large yellow onion, sliced
¼ cup Extra Light Olive Oil
1 teaspoon Himalayan Pink salt
½ teaspoon freshly ground black pepper
1 medium sized carrot, cubed
1 head Napa cabbage, quartered
1 teaspoon whole peppercorns
4 cups water

Directions:
Select "Sauté." When the display shows "Hot," add the oil.
Add chorizo de bilbao and bacon and sauté until bacon is crispy.
Press "Cancel."
Add onion, whole peppercorns, beef short ribs, water and tomato sauce.
Close and lock the lid. Set the vent to "sealing."
Select "Pressure Cook," High pressure, 45 minutes, "Warm" off.
When the display shows "Off," perform the NPR method and wait 10 minutes.
Follow the QR method to release any residual pressure and steam.
Wait until the pressure indicator pin drops down.

Carefully open and remove the lid.

Add carrots, Garbanzo beans, and bell pepper.

Close and lock the lid. Set the vent to "sealing."

Select "Pressure Cook," High pressure, 4 minutes, "Warm" off.

When the display shows "Off," perform the NPR method and wait 5 minutes.

Follow the QR method to release any residual pressure and steam.

Wait until the pressure indicator pin drops down.

Carefully open and remove the lid.

Select "Warm" and stir in cabbage and stir-cook until cabbage is wilted.

Select "Cancel."

Remove all to serving dish.

Add salt and pepper as you may desire.

Serve.

6.8. Longganisa Fried Rice

Ingredients:
1 tablespoon Avocado oil

1 lb. ground longganisa sausage

1 medium yellow onion, diced

2 medium carrots, peeled and finely chopped

1 green bell pepper, cored, seeded, finely chopped

4 cloves garlic, crushed, minced

3 cups cooked Basmati rice, cold

1 cup frozen peas, defrosted (optional)

2 tablespoons low-sodium soy sauce

1 large egg, beaten

1 green onion, thinly biased sliced

Directions:
Select "Sauté," "More." When the display shows "Hot", add the oil.

Add longganisa and cook until no longer pink. Use a wooden spatula to break up clumps.

Add onions, carrots and bell pepper and stir-fry until onion is translucent.

Add garlic and stir-fry 30 seconds.

Push all up the sides of the Instant Pot®.

Add the egg and let cook until almost completely set.

Using a wooden spatula, chop the eggs into strips.

Stir in rice, soy sauce, green onions and peas.

Stir-cook all together to mix thoroughly.

Select "Cancel."

Remove to a serving bowl.

Serves 4.

6.9. Subtle Chili Beef

Ingredients:
1 lb. beef Chouriço
3 tablespoons Grapeseed oil, divided
3 tablespoons low-sodium soy sauce
1 tablespoon Chinese rice wine
1 tablespoon cornstarch
2 teaspoons golden brown sugar
1 cup drained canned baby corn
1– 4 oz. can sliced water chestnuts, drained
3 green onions cut into 1 inch pieces
1 piece fresh ginger (1 inch), peeled, minced
2 cloves garlic, minced
¼ red bell pepper, cored, seeded, julienned
1 Habanero pepper, stem removed, seeded, and cut into strips
1 teaspoon hot chili oil
Hot cooked rice

Directions:
Cut steak lengthwise in half, then across the grain into ¼ inch-thick slices. Combine 1 tablespoon Grapeseed oil, soy sauce, wine, cornstarch and brown sugar in medium bowl. Add beef and toss to coat; set aside.
Select "Sauté," "More." When the display shows "Hot," add the oil. Stir-fry beef in batches until browned. Add additional oil as desired. Place cooked beef on platter.
Stir-fry corn, green onions, ginger, water chestnuts and garlic, 1 minute. Add bell pepper and Habanero and stir-fry 1 minute. Return beef and any juices to Instant Pot®.
Add chili oil. Toss until heated through.
Select "Cancel."
Serve over hot cooked rice.
Serves 4

6.10. Beef Short Ribs Sinigang

Ingredients:
1 lb. bone-in beef short ribs
1 enormous yellow onion, chopped
1 (½ inch) piece fresh ginger, peeled, chopped
2 plump Beefsteak tomatoes, peeled, cored, seeded, cut into ½ inch dice
2 cups water
1 – 1.41 oz. package Knorr® tamarind soup base
½ lb. fresh broccoli, trimmed
Yellow chile peppers

Directions:
Wash meat three times under cool water.
Put water, meat, tomatoes, ginger, and onions in the Instant Pot®.
Add one packet of Knorr® tamarind soup base.
Close and lock the lid. Set the vent to "sealing."
Select "Pressure Cook," High pressure, 45 minutes, "Warm" off.
When the display shows "Off," perform the NPR method and wait 10 minutes. Follow the QR method to release any residual pressure and steam.
Wait until the pressure indicator pin drops down.
Carefully open and remove the lid.
Add the vegetable*.
Simmer until vegetable* is tender
Don't overcook the vegetable*.
You can add a yellow chile pepper if you want spicy.

*Vegetable – broccoli, or Kangkong leaves, radish, taro, green beans.

6.11. Arroz Valencia

Ingredients:

½ lb. boneless, skinless chicken thigh, chopped in bite-sized pieces

Juice of 1 lemon

4 pieces chorizo de bilbao, sliced diagonally

½ cup malagkit (glutinous white rice)

1 cup Basmati rice

2 tablespoons tomato paste

1 medium red bell pepper, cored, seeded, julienned

½ cup golden raisins

½ cup frozen green peas

1 teaspoon sweet Hungarian paprika

2 cups low-sodium chicken broth

1 cup coconut milk

1 medium tomato, skinned, cored, seeded, diced

1 medium yellow onion, diced

6 garlic cloves, crushed, minced

3 large hard-boiled eggs, sliced

3 tablespoons Avocado oil

⅛ teaspoon Kashmiri saffron

Salt and freshly ground white pepper as you may desire

Directions:

Wash the chicken with lemon juice. Rinse and pat dry with paper towels.

Place the Basmati rice in a fine mesh strainer.

Using your fingers, gently rub the grains under running water to remove excess gluten.

Rinse, then drain.

Remove washed rice to a mixing bowl and blend with the glutinous rice. Set aside.

Select "Sauté," "More".

When the display shows "Hot", add the oil.

Sauté the onion until translucent.

Add the garlic and sauté 30 seconds.

Add the bell pepper and stir-cook until softened.

Fold in the tomato and stir-cook until tomato becomes soft.

Blend in the chicken and stir-cook for 3 minutes.

Add the chorizo de bilbao and stir-cook for 3 more minutes.

Scatter the salt, pepper, saffron, and paprika over the chicken. Stir until fragrant.

Add the broth and coconut milk.

Bring to a rolling boil.

Fold in the washed rice and tomato paste.

Stir to combine, then cover, select "Cancel," then "Warm," and simmer 10 minutes.

Fold in the raisins and green peas. Cover and simmer another 10 minutes.

When the rice and the chicken are cooked, garnish with sliced eggs and serve.

Select "Cancel."

6.12. Indian Sinagag

Ingredients:
1 tablespoon Avocado oil
¼ teaspoon mustard seeds
¼ cup diced white onion
6 garlic cloves, crushed, chopped
¼ teaspoon bird's eye chiles
2 cups of day-old cooked rice
1 tablespoon low sodium soy sauce
¼ cup canned sweet corn, drained
½ teaspoon turmeric

Directions:
Select "Sauté." When the display shows "Hot", add the oil.
Sprinkle mustard seeds over the oil.
When seeds begin to crackle, fold in onions and stir-cook until translucent.
Toss in the garlic and chiles and stir-cook 30 seconds.
Blend in rice, using a wooden spatula to break up clumps.
Drizzle soy sauce over the rice mixture and stir-cook to combine.
Fold in corn and stir-cook until all are heated through.
Broadcast turmeric over the rice mixture.
Using a spatula, stir-cook to mix the turmeric thoroughly with the rice mixture.
When the rice is a nice yellow color, remove from heat and mound on a serving platter.
Select "Cancel."
Serves 4.

Note: Substitute for "day-old cooked rice", freshly cooked rice, cooled under running cold water until rice reaches room temperature.

6.13. Garlic Fried Rice

Ingredients:
1 cup cooked Basmati rice
¼ teaspoon garlic powder
1 teaspoon salt, or as you may desire

Directions:
Select "Sauté," "More." When the display shows "Hot," add the oil.
Stir in the rice, using a wooden spatula to break up clumps.
Dust with the garlic powder and salt.
Stir-fry until rice is mixed and heated through.
Remove rice to a serving dish.
Select "Cancel."

6.14. Spanish Garlic Soup

Ingredients:
1 tablespoon Avocado oil
6 cloves garlic, very thinly sliced
2 ounces Longaanisa Hamonado, diced
1 tablespoon sweet Hungarian paprika (reserve a little for garnish)
¼ teaspoon hot Hungarian paprika
6 cups cubed stale French bread
6 cups low-sodium chicken broth
Finely ground Himalayan Pink salt and freshly ground black pepper as you may desire
¼ cup chopped fresh flat-leaf parsley, divided
4 large eggs

Directions:
Select "Sauté." When the display shows "Hot," add the oil.
Stir-cook garlic in hot oil until just golden.
Add ham and stir-cook until heated through, about 1 minute.
Fold in the paprikas. Stir until paprikas are fragrant.
Stir bread into Instant Pot® and toss to coat with paprika and garlic mixture. Pour chicken broth over bread mixture;
Stir in salt and black pepper as you may desire.
Bring to a boil, then select "Cancel," then select "Warm."
Stir in parsley. Crack each egg into a small bowl or cup.
Pour eggs into soup, equally spaced and not touching each other. Cover the pot and cook until eggs are poached firm but not cooked through.
Select "Cancel."
Divide soup among 4 bowls.
Gently place an egg in the center of each bowl.
Sprinkle with reserved sweet paprika and parsley.
Serves 4

6.15. Pinoy Hot and Sour Soup

Ingredients:
½ lb. pork shoulder, thinly sliced
1½ cups Shiitake mushrooms, sliced
½ cup dried wood ear, soaked in water 20 minutes
2 inch long piece of ginger, peeled, thinly sliced
4 pieces extra firm tofu, cubed
½ cup carrots, julienned
½ cup bamboo shoots, sliced
8 cups low-sodium chicken broth
½ cup rice vinegar
3 tablespoons low-sodium soy sauce
2 teaspoons Filipino sweet chili sauce
¼ teaspoon crushed red pepper flakes
3½ tablespoons Tapioca, dissolved in 4 tablespoons water
1 large egg, beaten
2 green onions, finely chopped
1 garlic clove, crushed, minced

Directions:
Drain the wood ear mushrooms and place in your Instant Pot®. Discard soaking water.
Add Shiitake mushrooms, ginger, pork, tofu, carrots, and bamboo shoots. Stir in soy sauce, rice vinegar, pepper flakes, garlic, and chili sauce.
Close and lock the lid. Set the vent to "sealing."
Select "Pressure Cook," High pressure, 15 minutes, "Warm" off. When the display shows "Off," perform the NPR method and wait 10 minutes. Follow the QR method to release any residual pressure and steam.
Wait until the pressure indicator pin drops down.
Carefully open and remove the lid.
Select "Sauté." When soup begins to boil, stir.

While stirring the soup, drizzle in the egg in a thin stream.
Stir in cornstarch and stir while the soup thickens.
Select "Cancel."
Ladle the soup into individual serving bowls and garnish with green onions.
Serves 8.

6.16. Hot and Sour Ramen Soup

Ingredients:
¼ cup longganisa sausage, casings removed
2 – 3 oz. dry ramen noodle bundles
5 cups water
2 oz. canned organic sliced mushrooms, drained
1 garlic clove, crushed, minced
2 tablespoons rice vinegar
¼ teaspoon Filipino sweet chili sauce
¼ teaspoon crushed red pepper flakes
2 green onions, thinly sliced
2 tablespoons Tapioca, dissolved in 4 tablespoons water(optional)

Directions:
Select "Sauté".
When the display shows "Hot", add the longganisa and stir-cook until cooked through.
Use a wooden spatula to break up clumps and to scrape up any burned bits.
Add the water and bring to boiling.
Stir in the ramen noodle bundles, garlic, and mushrooms.
Stir in vinegar, chili sauce, red pepper flakes, and green onions.
When the noodles are done to your liking, select "Cancel."
Stir in dissolved Tapioca powder until desired consistency is reached (optional).
Transfer to a soup tureen and serve.

7. Desserts and Toppings

7.1. Chocolate Mocha Cake

Ingredients:
2 cups all-purpose flour
2 cups white sugar
⅔ cup unsweetened cocoa powder
½ cup vegetable oil
2 eggs
1 cup buttermilk
1 teaspoon baking powder
2 teaspoons baking soda
½ teaspoon salt
1 tablespoon instant coffee powder
1½ cup water
Coffee Icing
4 squares, semisweet chocolate

Directions:
Grease two 9 inch round springform cake pans.
Measure flour, sugar, cocoa, oil, eggs, buttermilk, baking powder, soda, and salt into a mixing bowl. Dissolve instant coffee in hot water, and add to mixing bowl.
Beat at medium speed for 2 minutes until smooth; batter will be thin.
Pour into prepared pans. Cover each pan with foil.
Pour water into your Instant Pot® and place a trivet at the bottom.
Place one of the covered pans on the trivet. Carefully place the other pan on top.
Close and lock the lid. Set the vent to "sealing."
Select "Pressure Cook," High pressure, 35 minutes, "Warm" off.
When the display shows "Off," perform the NPR method and wait 10 minutes.

Follow the QR method to release any residual pressure and steam.

Wait until the pressure indicator pin drops down.

Carefully open and remove the lid.

Carefully remove pans and quickly remove foil so water residue on top doesn't fall on your cakes.

Cool in pans for 10 minutes, and then turn out onto racks to cool completely.

Frost cooled cakes with Coffee Icing.

After frosting, melt some semisweet chocolate baking squares or chips in a double boiler.

Drizzle chocolate around top outside edges letting it run over top and down sides of cake.

7.2. Puto (Steamed Rice Cake)

Ingredients:
1 cup rice flour
1 tablespoon baking powder
½ cup sugar
2 cups water

Directions:
In a 2 quart mixing bowl, mix together flour, baking powder, sugar, and 1 cup water.

Pour batter into ceramic ramekins or small pyrex® bowls.

Add remaining water to Instant Pot®.

Place trivet in Instant Pot® and arrange ramekins on trivet.

Close and lock the lid. Set the vent to "sealing."

Press "Steam", High pressure, 15 minutes, "Warm" off.

When the display shows "Off," perform the NPR method and wait 10 minutes.

Follow the QR method to release any residual pressure and steam.

Wait until the pressure indicator pin drops down.

Carefully open and remove the lid.

Remove ramekins from steamer and let cool completely.

7.3. Bibingka

Ingredients:
2 cups rice flour
1 cup light brown sugar
1 tablespoon baking powder
3 eggs, beaten
3 tablespoons unsalted butter, melted
1 –14 oz. container coconut milk
1 banana leaf, washed (optional)
2 cups water
1 tablespoon unsalted butter, sliced
2 tablespoons fresh (or frozen) grated coconut

Directions:
Line an 8X3 inch round springform baking pan with parchment paper.
Alternatively, line pan with banana leaf, (if using) cut according to the size of the pan
[The banana leaf adds a traditional fragrance to the cake when cooked.]
In a bowl, combine the first 6 ingredients with 1 cup water.
Mix thoroughly to form a smooth batter.
Pour batter mixture into prepared pan. Cover with aluminum foil.
Pour remaining water into the Instant Pot®.
Place a trivet in the Instant Pot®. Place the cake on the trivet.
Close and lock the lid. Set the vent to "sealing."
Select "Pressure Cook," High pressure, 35 minutes, "Warm" off.
When the display shows "Off," perform the NPR method and wait 10 minutes.
Follow the QR method to release any residual pressure and steam.

Wait until the pressure indicator pin drops down.

Carefully open and remove the lid.

Remove pan and quickly remove foil so water residue on top doesn't fall on your cakes

Cool in pan for 10 minutes, and then turn out onto rack to cool completely.

Place the cake on a serving platter and put butter slices on top. Sprinkle with grated coconut.

7.4. Bibingka Espesyal

Ingredients:
2 cups all-purpose flour (or rice flour)
2 teaspoons baking powder
1 teaspoon salt
3 eggs
1 cup sugar
1¼ cups coconut milk
1 cup water
¼ cup grated (sharp) cheddar cheese
2 tablespoons melted butter
2 tablespoons white cane sugar
For serving:
½ cup grated fresh coconut

Directions:
Line two 8 inch springform baking pans with parchment paper.
In a bowl, sift flour, baking powder and salt together. Set aside.
In another bowl, beat the eggs until light and creamy.
Gradually add sugar (about ¼ cup at a time) beating well after each addition (about 5 minutes).
Alternate adding flour mixture and coconut milk.
Beat to blend thoroughly.
Pour mixture in lined pans. Cover with aluminum foil.
Pour water into the Instant Pot®.
Place a trivet in the Instant Pot®. Place the cake on the trivet.
Close and lock the lid. Set the vent to "sealing."
Select "Pressure Cook," High pressure, 15 minutes, "Warm" off.
When the display shows "Off," perform the NPR method and wait 10 minutes.

Follow the QR method to release any residual pressure and steam.

Wait until the pressure indicator pin drops down.

Carefully open and remove the lid.

Carefully remove pan and quickly remove foil so water residue on top doesn't fall on your cakes.

While still hot, sprinkle top of cake with grated (sharp) cheddar cheese.

Brush top with butter and sprinkle with sugar.

Serve with grated fresh coconut.

7.5. Polvoron

Ingredients:
2 cups all-purpose flour
1 cup powdered milk
1 cup sugar
½ cup melted butter

non-stick muffin pan

Directions:
Select "Sauté." When the display shows "Hot," add the flour and stir-cook until lightly brown.
Add powdered milk and continue stirring for another 5 minutes.
Select "Cancel."
Remove toasted flour and milk mixture to a suitable mixing bowl and let cool.
When cool, combine toasted flour and milk mixture with sugar and butter.
When the mixture becomes like damp sand, spoon into paper cups in muffin pan
Press firmly to consolidate.

7.6. Kutsinta

Ingredients:
1 cup rice flour
¾ cup brown sugar
½ teaspoon Lye Water
2½ cups water, divided
For serving:
homemade Latik (recipe follows)
grated coconut

Directions:
In a non-reactive bowl, whisk first three ingredients with 1½ cup water.
Pour batter into ceramic ramekins or small pyrex® bowls.
Pour batter mixture into prepared pan. Cover with aluminum foil.
Pour remaining water into the Instant Pot®.
Place a trivet in the Instant Pot®. Arrange the ramekins on the trivet.
Close and lock the lid. Set the vent to "sealing."
Select "Pressure Cook," High pressure, 15 minutes, "Warm" off.
When the display shows "Off," perform the NPR method and wait 10 minutes. Follow the QR method to release any residual pressure and steam.
Wait until the pressure indicator pin drops down.
Carefully open and remove the lid.
Carefully remove ramekins and quickly remove foil so water residue on top doesn't fall on your cakes.
Place ramekins on a wire rack to cool completely.
Using a butter knife, release the kutsinta from the ramekins.
Sprinkle Latik and coconut over each.
Serve.

Homemade Latik
Ingredients:
1–14 oz. can coconut milk

Directions:
In a non-reactive pot, bring coconut milk to a boil. Reduce heat to simmer.

Stirring frequently, simmer the coconut milk until milk thickens.

Continue stirring until coconut oil separates from deposited solids or crumbs.

Continue stirring until crumbs turn a deep caramel color.

Remove from heat and pour off the coconut oil.

Reserve the dark crumbs.

7.7. Banana Cue (Barbekyung Saging)

Ingredients:
2 tablespoons Avocado oil
16 semi ripe "Saba" bananas, peeled, cut in half, lengthwise
½ cup white cane sugar

Directions:
Select "Sauté." When the display shows "Hot," add the oil and heat to shimmering.
Add the bananas and fry and flip until they become golden brown.
Using a wire strainer, remove to a paper towel-covered plate. Select "Cancel."
In another rimmed plate, pour sugar.
Add bananas, one at a time, turning to coat with sugar.
Arrange coated bananas on a serving plate.
Enjoy!

7.8. Pinaypay

Ingredients:
6 pieces ripe "Saba" banana
1 cup all-purpose flour
½ teaspoon salt as you may desire
¾ cup granulated white sugar, divided
1 egg, beaten
1½ teaspoon vanilla extract
1 cup fresh milk
2 tablespoons Avocado oil

Directions:
In a large bowl, combine flour, salt, and ½ cup sugar. Mix well.
Add the egg, vanilla extract, and milk.
Mix to incorporate all the ingredients.
Using a paring knife, make 4-5 slices vertically down half the length of the banana.
Spread the slices to form a fan.
Select "Sauté." When the display shows "Hot," add the oil and heat to shimmering.
Dip banana fan in the batter, and coat both sides.
Carefully lower the fan into the hot oil.
Fry both sides until the color turns golden brown.
Drain on paper towels.
Dredge in sugar while still warm. Shake off excess.
Repeat until all bananas are cooked.
Select "Cancel."
Serves 6

7.9. Biko

Ingredients:
2 cups glutinous rice (aka sticky rice or malagkit)
1½ cups water
1 cup brown sugar
2 cups coconut milk
For serving:
¼ cup dried coconut flakes

Directions:
Select "Warm." Ste the time to 10 minutes.
When the display shows 2 minutes have elapsed add butter and melt.
Add the sticky rice and stir to coat.
Select "Cancel."
Add water, sugar, and coconut milk.
Close and lock the lid. Set the vent to "sealing."
Select "Pressure Cook," High pressure, 12 minutes, "Warm" off.
When the display shows "Off," perform the NPR method and wait 10 minutes.
Follow the QR method to release any residual pressure and steam.
Wait until the pressure indicator pin drops down.
Carefully open and remove the lid.
Remove Biko from pot to a square glass baking dish lined with parchment paper.
Cool, dust with coconut flakes, cut into squares, and serve.
Makes 8 servings.

7.10. Fried Pineapple

Ingredients:
1 whole ripe pineapple
¼ cup white cane sugar
2 tablespoons unsalted butter
¼ cup golden raisins
2 oz. bittersweet chocolate, shaved
Fresh mint leaves for garnish

Directions:
Using a sharp knife, slice the top off of the pineapple.
Using a pineapple slicer tool, core and slice the pineapple into rings.
Spread sugar on a plate and dredge the pineapple rings in the sugar.
Select "Sauté." When the display shows "Hot," add butter and melt.
Cooking them in batches, fry the dredged pineapple rings for 2 minutes.
Flip the rings and spread raisins around them.
Brown the pineapple rings.
Remove from heat.
Select "Cancel."
Arrange the fried pineapple rings, browned side up, on dessert plates.
Spoon some cooked raisins over it.
Spoon some raisins onto each plate and top with the sauce from the pan.
Garnish with chocolate shavings and mint.
Serves 10

8. Sauces

8.1. Red Curry Paste

Ingredients:
1 teaspoon garam marsala powder
½ teaspoon freshly ground white pepper
1 large red bell pepper, cored, seeded, chopped
½ teaspoon bird's eye chiles
1 stalk lemongrass, thinly sliced
⅛ teaspoon ginger powder
¼ teaspoon garlic powder
¼ teaspoon Himalayan Pink salt
1 teaspoon turmeric powder
6 green onions, thinly sliced
1 tablespoon Avocado oil
1 tablespoon white cane sugar
1 teaspoon lemon juice
1 teaspoon lime juice

Directions:
Place all ingredients in a food processor.
Pulse to form a smooth paste.
Remove to a sealed container and refrigerate

8.2. Pinoy BBQ Sauce

Ingredients:
1 cup rice vinegar
1 tablespoon low-sodium soy sauce
2 tablespoons light brown sugar
2 tablespoons banana ketchup
1 teaspoon crushed red pepper flakes
1 tablespoon bourbon whiskey
2 teaspoons fish sauce
¼ teaspoon Chinese 5 spice powder
1 teaspoon salt
1 teaspoon black pepper
Juice and zest of 1 lime

Directions:
Combine all ingredients in a saucepan and stir-cook until sugar is dissolved.
Let cool and store in a wide mouthed jar.

8.3. Easy Balsamic Vinaigrette

Ingredients:
¼ cup sweet Balsamic vinegar (at least 9 gms. sugar per serving)
1 cup extra-virgin olive oil
⅛ teaspoon Xanthan Gum powder
½ teaspoon calamansi juice

Directions:
Pour Balsamic vinegar into a sealable bottle or 12 oz. cruet with seal.
Add olive oil, calamansi juice, seal and shake until the contents are well mixed.
Add Xanthan Gum powder.
Seal and shake until Xanthan Gum powder is dissolved.

Tip: for added flavor, add 1 crushed and minced garlic clove

8.4. Homemade Piri Piri Sauce

Ingredients:
1 cup bird's eye peppers, coarsely chopped
6 cloves garlic, crushed, minced
1 medium onion, finely chopped
1 tablespoon sweet Hungarian paprika
¼ teaspoon hot Hungarian paprika
2 tablespoons tomato paste
1 tablespoon Jufran® Banana Sauce
1 teaspoon Himalayan Pink salt
1 cup extra-light olive oil
¼ cup white wine vinegar

Directions:
Place all ingredients in a food processor and combine until smooth.

8.5. Salsa Verde Cruda

Ingredients:
10 medium tomatillos, husked and washed
2 serrano chiles, cored
½ small onion, chopped
¼ cup water
½ teaspoon salt (optional)

Directions:
Boil fresh tomatillos in salted water to cover until barely tender, and drain.
Place the tomatillos in a food processor.
If you want a milder sauce, seed the chile(s), then chop into small bits.
Add to the tomatillos along with the chopped onion.
Pulse to a coarse puree.
Scrape into a sauce dish.
Add water to thin to a medium-thick consistency.
Season with salt as you may desire.
Let stand for about ½ hour before serving so the flavors can blend.
Yield: 6 Servings

9. Filipino Ingredient Substitutes

Achuete, atsuete, 1 tbsp. .. ⅛ tsp. red food coloring or (used in pancit molo) .. 2 tsp. paprika
Bulaklak ng saging …. dried lily blossoms available at most Chinese stores
Chorizo de Bilbao …. Pepperoni, garlic sausage or oxford sausage
Gabi ….. Yam
Calamansi ….. Lime or Lemon
Kamias ….. Lemon juice or rhubarb
Kangkong …… Watercress or spinach
Labanos ….. Red or white radish
isua …… Very fine noodles (vermicelli)
Singkamas ……. Turnips
Talbos ng Ampalaya …… Watercress or spinach
Talbos ng sili ….. Spinach

10. A Final Note

MABUHAY!!

Hey everybody, just wanted to say **THANK YOU** again for checking out my book.

I hope you enjoyed "**Filipino Instant Pot® Cooking!**" as much as I did preparing it.

These recipes were selected coming from my heart, and put together with love.

Enjoy them and Salamat Po. (thank you).

Just a final thought: There is a Filipino tradition: after the party and there's some food left over, the guests can take the food home! We call it "baon" -'to go'.

If you enjoyed my book, won't you please take a moment to leave me a review at your favorite retailer?

Thanks!

---

11. Bonus Recipes

A hearty "Thank You Very Much" - *Salamat Po* - to all my fantastic and faithful followers. It has given me great pleasure to both share these fun and tasty recipes with you, and to read the heart-warming response from those brave souls who, although not Filipinos, have tried and found they actually enjoy our Island cooking.

As with all down-to-earth foods, Filipino fare is easy to prepare, uses wholesome and nourishing ingredients, and can be fun to make when approached with the correct attitude.

Most people are afraid to make a mistake, either in cooking or in life. To them, I say, "Try it! Make something that you've never tried before. Don't worry if it turns out not to your liking, or as if you thought it should. Go ahead! Try it again!!"

I never worry about throwing out something that has failed: I just go out, get more ingredients and try again. That's the only way you'll learn.

Some of these seemingly easy recipes here are the result of many hours of failed experiments. But the end results have been amazing! Look at what you're holding in your hands.

So, go ahead. Try your hand at it. After all Paris wasn't built in a fortnight!!

Warmly,

Lola Nita Concepcion

11.1. Chicken Inasal

Ingredients:
For the *Atsuete* oil (makes ½ cup):
½ cup Grapeseed oil
⅛ cup atsuete seeds
2 cloves garlic, crushed, minced
½ bay leaf
1 dried ancho chile, crushed, stemmed, seeded
For the Chicken:
¼ cup atsuete oil
3 garlic cloves, finely chopped
1 stalk lemongrass, trimmed and finely chopped
3 tablespoons freshly squeezed calamansi or lime juice
2 tablespoons cider vinegar
1 tablespoon golden brown sugar
2 teaspoon salt as you may desire
1 teaspoon finely chopped fresh ginger
¼ teaspoon freshly ground white pepper as you may desire
1 – 3½ pound chicken, quartered or cut into pieces
Avocado oil

Directions:
To Make the Atsuete oil:
Heat a non-reactive deep sidewall saucepan over medium heat.
Add all of the Atsuete ingredients.
Bring to a rolling boil, cover, and remove from heat.
Allow to rest for 1 to 2 hours.
Filter the oil through a coffee filter.
Let cool.
Store in an airtight container in the refrigerator.

To Marinate the Chicken:

In a large non-reactive bowl, combine all the marinade ingredients.

Pour mixture into a freezer zipper-locked plastic bag.

Cut deep slits into the chicken pieces then add to the bag.

Seal bag, and knead to make sure marinade covers the chicken.

Refrigerate for at least 1 hour, preferably overnight.

To Cook the Chicken:

Preheat grill to 550°F.

Brush the chicken with Avocado oil and place on grill.

Baste with marinade and flip until done.

Serve with garlic rice and chili-infused vinegar.

11.2. Bistecca Con Salsa delle Erbe

Ingredients:
1 cup packed basil leaves
1 cup packed flat-leaf parsley leaves
2 tablespoons packed fresh oregano leaves
1 tablespoon packed fresh rosemary leaves
1 tablespoon packed fresh thyme leaves
1 tablespoon packed fresh tarragon leaves
2 cloves garlic, minced
¾ cup plus 2 tablespoon extra-light olive oil, divided
Kosher salt and freshly ground black pepper, to taste
1 – 24 oz., 2 –3 inch-thick rib-eye, strip, or porterhouse steak

Directions:
Chop the herbs and garlic in a food processor.
Add ¾ cup oil and blend to a fine paste.
Season with salt and pepper to taste.
Cover tightly and let rest for at least an hour at room temperature.
Coat both sides of steak with the remaining oil, and heavily dust with salt and pepper.
On a well-seasoned and oiled grill over medium high heat, cook the steak as you like it.
Using tongs, turn steak only once.
(cook 8–10 minutes on a side for medium rare)
Transfer steak to a serving platter, cover, and let rest for 5 minutes.
Slice steak against the grain.
Arrange on a serving platter and ladle the herb blend over the meat.
Serves 2

11.3. Bistecca alla Fiorentina

Ingredients:
1½ lb. T-bone or Porterhouse steak, cut from the rib with the bone.
2 tablespoons extra light olive oil
Sea salt and freshly ground pepper, to taste
Lemon wedges for garnish
1½ cups baby arugula

Directions:
Take the meat out of the refrigerator about 2 hours before cooking it.
Prepare a charcoal or gas grill for direct grilling over medium-high heat.
Brush the meat on both sides with the oil. (Do not add any salt at this point.)
Using tongs, lay the steak directly over the hottest part of the fire, about 5 inches above the fire.
Cook until browned and juicy on the first side, 5 to 7 minutes.
Using tongs, turn the steak and sprinkle with salt.
Cook on the second side until browned and juicy, 5 to 7 minutes more.
Then turn the meat over once again and sprinkle with salt.
Transfer the steak to a cutting board and season generously with pepper.
Let rest 5 minutes, covered.
Garnish with lemon wedges and the arugula and serve immediately.
Serves 2.

11.4. Pancetta-finished Clams Casino

Ingredients:
Cooking spray
¾ cup finely diced pancetta
2 tablespoons dry white wine (drinking wine, NOT "cooking" wine – too much salt)
⅓ cup finely diced red bell pepper, cored seeded
3 tablespoons minced shallots
1 garlic clove, minced
¾ cup Italian Panko breadcrumbs
1½ tablespoons grated fresh Parmigiano-Reggiano cheese
2 teaspoons finely chopped fresh parsley
¼ teaspoon freshly ground white pepper
36 live littleneck clams, cleaned
Lemon wedges as may be desired
Cocktail sauce as may be desired

Directions:
Heat a medium skillet over medium heat.
Coat skillet with cooking spray.
Add pancetta to skillet.
Cook 6 minutes or until pancetta begins to brown, stirring occasionally.
Add wine; cook until liquid evaporates, scraping skillet to loosen browned bits.
Add bell pepper, shallots, and garlic to pancetta.
Cook 4 minutes or until tender.
Place pancetta mixture in a medium bowl.
Add breadcrumbs, cheese, parsley, and white pepper to pancetta mixture.
Stir gently until blended.

Preheat oven broiler.

Discard any clams with broken or open shells.

Shuck clams and discard top halves of shells.

Place cleaned clams in a single layer in a shallow baking pan.

Top each clam with about 1 rounded teaspoon pancetta mixture.

Broil 4 minutes. Adjust pan.

Broil an additional 3 minutes or until tops are browned and clams are done.

Serve with lemon wedges and cocktail sauce, if desired.

11.5. Cotes de Porc Sauce Moutarde

Ingredients:
4 pork chops
1 tablespoon salt
1 tablespoon freshly ground white pepper
2 tablespoons butter
2 tablespoons Dijon mustard
½ cup water
3 tablespoons whipping cream or crème fraîche

Directions:
In a shallow dish, combine salt and pepper.
Liberally rub the pork chops with salt and pepper on all sides.
In a non-reactive deep sided skillet, melt the butter until just foaming.
Add the pork chops but don't crowd the pan.
Brown on each side about 2 minutes.
Mix the water into the mustard and pour on top of the pork chops.
Cover and cook on low heat until pork chops are done, 15 to 20 minutes.
Remove pork chops.
Cook sauce, uncovered, over high heat until reduced by about half.
Remove skillet from heat.
Stir in cream and blend thoroughly.
Pour sauce on pork chops and serve.
Serves 4

11.6. BBQ Chicken Drumsticks

Ingredients:
8 chicken drumsticks, bone in, skin on
Dry rub:
2 tablespoons brown sugar
2 teaspoons each: sweet Hungarian paprika, garlic powder, Lawry's® Salt Free 17 Seasonings
2 teaspoons each: onion powder, black pepper, dry mustard
½ teaspoon cayenne pepper, optional
For cooking:
1 cup water
Aluminum foil, cut into 6 inch squares
2 cups your favorite BBQ sauce, plus more for serving

Directions:
In a medium mixing bowl blend the dry rub ingredients together.
With your hands, massage the dry rub evenly into the meat on all sides of the drumsticks.
Place a trivet in your Instant Pot®.
Pour the water into your Instant Pot®.
Arrange the drumsticks on the trivet and brush the BBQ sauce over all.
Place a square of aluminum foil between layers of drumsticks.
Close and lock the lid. Set the steam valve to "sealing."
Select "Pressure Cook," High pressure, 10 minutes, "Warm" off.
When the display shows "Off," perform the NPR method and wait 10 minutes.
Perform the QR method, releasing any residual pressure and steam.
Wait until the pressure indicator pin drops down, then carefully open the lid.

Remove drumsticks to a serving platter.
Serve immediately with a side of BBQ sauce as you may desire!

Note: Finish on a hot gas grill to make it look like these drumsticks were cooked outdoors! Baste with your favorite BBQ sauce during the grilling process.

11.7. Corned Beef

Ingredients:
1 large yellow onion, cut into wedges
1 – 2 lb. corned beef brisket, with seasoning packet
4 cups low-sodium chicken broth
1 small head cabbage, core removed and cut into wedges
1 lb. fingerling potatoes, halved
4 medium carrots, sliced and bias-cut
3 tablespoons Avocado olive oil
Kosher salt as you may desire
Freshly ground black pepper as you may desire
Freshly chopped parsley, for serving

Directions:
Place onion in bottom of the Instant Pot®.
Place brisket on top and add seasoning packet.
Pour in broth.
Close and lock the lid. Set the vent to "sealing."
Select "Pressure Cook," High pressure, 90 minutes, "Warm" off.
When the display shows "Off," perform the NPR method and wait 5 minutes.
Follow the QR method to release any residual pressure and steam.
Wait until the pressure indicator pin drops down.
Carefully open and remove the lid.
Remove corned beef and onions to a serving dish.
Retain the cooking liquid inside the Instant Pot®.
Cover beef and keep warm.
Add cabbage, potatoes, carrots, and oil to the Instant Pot®.
Season with salt and pepper as you may desire.
Close and lock the lid. Set the vent to "sealing."

Select "Pressure Cook," High pressure, 4 minutes, "Warm" off.

When the display shows "Off," perform the QR method to release any residual pressure and steam.

Wait until the pressure indicator pin drops down.

Carefully open and remove the lid.

Remove vegetables to a serving dish.

Serve vegetables with corned beef.

Pour cooking liquid through a fat separator.

Garnish with parsley and spoon the cooking liquid over beef, if desired.

12. About Lola Nita Concepcion

Lola Nita Concepcion is a native of Puerto Princesa, Palawan, Philippines.

Her well-deserved reputation as a legendary cook from the 'Old Country' comes from generations of famous Palawan cooks. Her recipes stretch back to the 16th century when Spain invaded the Islands. At one point, the Vice Regent of the Philippines was a guest in her great-great-grandmother's house, and her family's signature dish, 'Suckling Piglet with Apricots', was the talk of the Island Court for months.

13. Books by Lola Nita Concepcion

Please visit your favorite book retailer to discover other books by Lola Nita Concepcion.

Published:
Healthy Filipino Cooking: Back Home Comfort Food
Fresh and Healthy Filipino Food: A Nutritious Taste of Home in a Foreign Land
Diabetics Cook Filipino: Eat Healthy! Tasty Island Foods!
Filipino Street Foods for Busy People: YES! You CAN do it!
Easy and Nutritious Soup!
Filipino Fusion!
Fast and Easy Filipino Cooking for Busy People!

Upcoming In the Near Future:
Fresh Island Foods: Filipino at its Best

Books to Watch For:
Lola Nita's Best Recipes: Filipino Fare like you've never tasted it before

Made in the USA
San Bernardino, CA
23 November 2019

60352530R00083